Addison County's Finest
Vermont Recipes

Addison County's Finest
Vermont Recipes

Edited by Kimberly Werner
Illustrations by Todd Cummings

PALATINE BOOKS
in association with
THE ADDISON COUNTY CHAMBER OF COMMERCE

Published by
PALATINE BOOKS/ACCC
2 Court Street
Middlebury, Vermont 05753

Library of Congress Catalog Card Number: 95-68132

10 9 8 7 6 5 4 3 2

Printed and bound in the United States of America by
World Color Book Services
Taunton, Massachusetts

DESIGN BY JAMIE EVANS
PRODUCTION BY FUTURA DESIGN
RESEARCH BY DAVID K. SMITH

Contents

Introduction

A ddison County: The Land of Milk and Honey. So said the old county sign on the Brandon-Leicester border along Route 7. Though the sign is now gone, the bounty is still evident in this pastoral region of Vermont. Addison County is primarily a landscape of fertile agricultural land and extensive apple orchards. Products that are shipped to markets throughout the country are also transported to local farmers' markets just several miles away. Many area chefs tend to their own gardens and rely on homegrown produce for their recipes. Surrounding forests and fields also yield a number of indigenous products—patches of wild mushrooms, clumps of fiddlehead ferns, clusters of berries and, of course, the towering maple trees that are tapped to extract one of Vermont's most famous products, maple syrup.

Addison County

The recipes in this book have been collected from Addison County dining and lodging establishments and often reflect the abundance of local products. Cream of Butternut Squash Soup is sweetened with just a hint of maple syrup, Dilled Tomato Bisque is made from plump, homegrown tomatoes when in season, Raspberry Crumble Muffins are best when prepared with delicate wild raspberries, Polenta Timbale with Vermont Goat Cheese makes use of this by-product of the thriving Vermont dairy industry, Ragoût of Ramps & Fiddlehead Ferns depends on the dark green coiled fern fronds that are found in local woodlands for its unique flavor and Stewed Apples and Oatmeal Apple Raisin Muffins are simple but delicious recipes that make use of the local abundance of apples.

The region's recipes also reflect a host of diverse influences. There are hearty New England classics, recipes that have been passed from generation to generation—Orange-Ginger Pork Chops, Butternut Squash, Fruited

Baby Carrots, Sesame Seed Bread, Maple Walnut Muffins, Apple Bread, Sour Cream Coffeecake with Nut Topping, Pumpkin-Apple Streusel Muffins, Johnny Cake and Maple Oatmeal Pie. Innovative and classic American and international recipes include Broccoli & Cheddar Fritters, Stuffed Mushroom Caps, Fresh Fennel & Roasted Garlic Soup, Warm Shrimp Caesar Salad with Three Relishes, Smoked Chicken Salad with Walnut Dressing, Cornmeal-Crusted Goat Cheese Salad, Salmon with Strawberry & Black Peppercorn Vinaigrette, Lamb Chops with Herbal Cream Sauce, Grilled Swordfish with Mango Salsa, Lemon-Almond Pound Cake, Mud Pie, Sweet Chimichangas, Walnut Chocolate Chip Scones, Crêpes Mousseline, Lemon Kiwi Tart and Bananas Foster.

Twenty-seven dining and lodging establishments contributed a menu of their favorite recipes to this cookbook. By turning to the "Dining & Lodging Directory" on page 13 and referring to the map on the facing page, you will be able to see where each establishment is located within the county. The corresponding page numbers will direct you to the chapter devoted to each restaurant, hotel and bed and breakfast. Here, you will find a brief description of the establishment, a suggested menu as well as the recipes to prepare the menu.

Whether you are simply planning a meal or setting off on an adventure, this book will help you discover some of Addison County's finest recipes and the reasons why this corner of Vermont is so unique.

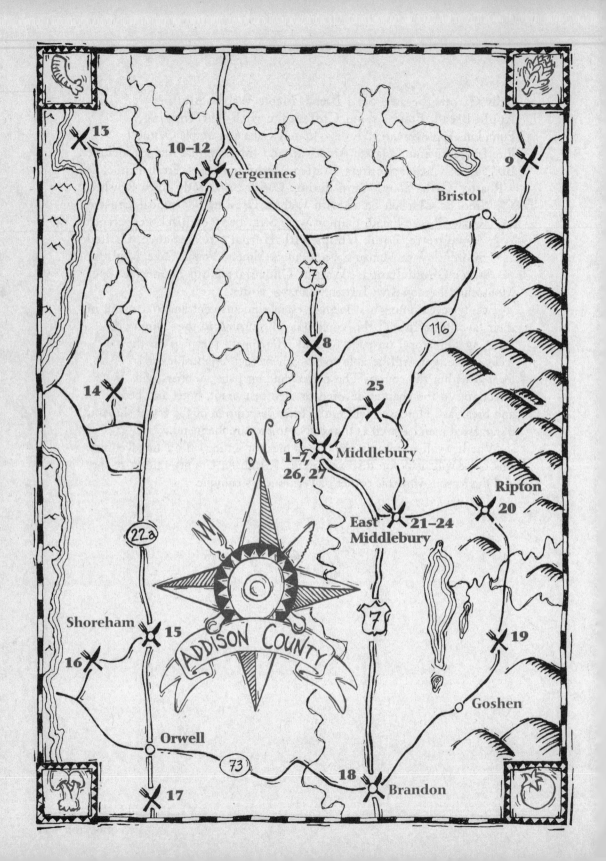

Dining & Lodging Directory

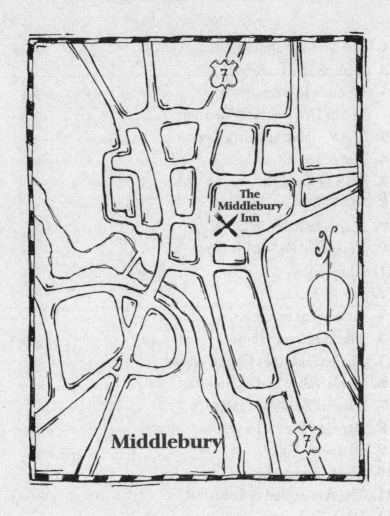

The
Middlebury
Inn

7

N

7

Middlebury

The Middlebury Inn

Court House Square
P.O. Box 798
Middlebury, Vermont 05753
(802) 388-4961/(800) 842-4666

ESTABLISHED IN 1827, this Middlebury landmark has welcomed guests for almost 170 years. The stately brick building, listed on the National Register of Historic Places, is a striking presence as it rises from the eastern border of the Village Green. Guests enjoy the warm hospitality, comfortable surroundings and plentiful New England fare for which the inn is known. In summer, guests may dine on the terrace overlooking the Green.

NEARBY & NOTEWORTHY: Just across from the inn's main entrance is the Gamaliel Painter House. This elegant colonial was built by the patron saint of Middlebury College in 1802. The building was recently restored and now houses the Addison County Chamber of Commerce and the Vermont Folklife Center, where you can learn about the folk art and traditions of Vermont.

Chilled Strawberry Soup

Village Greens

Seafood Gratinée

Carrot Casserole

Fanned Red Bliss Potatoes

Bananas Foster

Chilled Strawberry Soup

1   PINT STRAWBERRIES, HULLED
1   CUP SOUR CREAM
3   TABLESPOONS BRANDY
    SUGAR
2   CUPS HALF-AND-HALF

CHOP strawberries in a blender. Add sour cream, brandy and sugar to taste and puree. Stir in half-and-half. Chill the soup for at least 2 hours before serving.

MAKES 4 SERVINGS.

Village Greens

¼ CUP BALSAMIC VINEGAR

1 TEASPOON FINELY CHOPPED SHALLOTS

1 TEASPOON DIJON MUSTARD

¾ CUP EXTRA-VIRGIN OLIVE OIL

   SALT & FRESHLY GROUND BLACK PEPPER

6 CUPS WASHED AND DRIED MESCLUN (ARUGULA, CHERVIL, GREEN OAK LEAF LETTUCE, LOLLO ROSSA, MÂCHE, MIZUNA, RED OAK LEAF LETTUCE, TAT-SOI)

8 CHERRY TOMATOES, CUT IN HALF

1 CUP CROUTONS, PREFERABLY HOMEMADE

¼ POUND BLUE CHEESE, CRUMBLED

WHISK together vinegar, shallots and mustard in a large salad bowl. Add oil in a steady stream while continuing to whisk. Season with salt and pepper to taste. Add mesclun, tomatoes, croutons and blue cheese and toss well.

MAKES 4 SERVINGS.

Seafood Gratinée

Substituting canned lobster bisque for fresh will make this dish even easier to prepare.

LOBSTER BISQUE

2	TABLESPOONS LIGHTLY SALTED BUTTER
2	TABLESPOONS ALL-PURPOSE FLOUR
1	CUP LIGHT CREAM
⅛	POUND LOBSTER MEAT, CHOPPED
2	TABLESPOONS CREAM (SWEET) SHERRY
2	TABLESPOONS BRANDY

GRATINÉE

¼	POUND (1 STICK) LIGHTLY SALTED BUTTER, MELTED
1	POUND SEA SCALLOPS
12	LARGE SHRIMP, PEELED AND DEVEINED
½	POUND FRESH OR FROZEN MAINE LUMP CRABMEAT, SQUEEZED DRY
½	POUND LOBSTER MEAT (TAIL AND CLAW)
⅛	POUND CHEDDAR CHEESE, GRATED (½ CUP)
12	RITZ CRACKERS, CRUMBLED

TO PREPARE LOBSTER BISQUE: Melt butter in a small saucepan. Add flour and cook, whisking constantly, until smooth.

In another saucepan, bring cream, lobster, sherry and brandy almost to a boil over medium heat. Whisk in the flour mixture. Reduce heat to low. Simmer, stirring constantly, for 2 minutes. Remove from the heat.

TO PREPARE GRATINÉE: Preheat oven to 400 degrees F.

Divide melted butter, scallops and shrimp evenly among 4 baking dishes. Bake for 20 minutes.

Distribute crabmeat, lobster and the lobster bisque among the dishes. Sprinkle with Cheddar and cracker crumbs. Bake the gratinée until the Cheddar is melted and the cracker crumbs are browned, 5 to 10 minutes.

MAKES 4 SERVINGS.

Carrot Casserole

2	POUNDS CARROTS, CUT DIAGONALLY INTO ¼-INCH-THICK SLICES
¼	CUP GRATED ONIONS
1	CUP MAYONNAISE
1½	TEASPOONS BOTTLED HORSERADISH
1	TEASPOON SALT
½	TEASPOON GROUND BLACK PEPPER
12	RITZ CRACKERS, CRUMBLED
	PAPRIKA FOR GARNISH

PREHEAT oven to 375 degrees F. Butter a large baking dish.

Boil carrots in salted water to cover until just tender, about 5 minutes. Drain, reserving ½ cup of the cooking liquid.

Stir together onions, mayonnaise, horseradish, salt, pepper and the reserved cooking liquid. Stir in the carrots. Pour into the prepared baking dish and top with cracker crumbs and paprika. Bake the casserole until golden brown, 20 to 25 minutes.

MAKES 4 SERVINGS.

Fanned Red Bliss Potatoes

8	SMALL RED POTATOES
1	MEDIUM ONION, CUT INTO JULIENNE
2	CLOVES GARLIC, FINELY CHOPPED
2	TEASPOONS CHOPPED FRESH ROSEMARY
	SALT & GROUND BLACK PEPPER
¼	POUND (1 STICK) LIGHTLY SALTED BUTTER, CUT INTO BITS
2	CUPS CHICKEN STOCK, PREFERABLY HOMEMADE

MAKE a cut in the potatoes every ⅛ inch, taking care not to cut all the way through the base.

Arrange the potatoes in a skillet large enough to hold them in one layer. Sprinkle with onions, garlic and rosemary. Season with salt and pepper to taste. Distribute butter over the top. Add chicken stock and cover with aluminum foil. Cook over medium heat until the potatoes are tender, about 30 minutes.

To serve, place two potatoes on each plate. Press gently with a spoon to fan and top with the onion mixture.

MAKES 4 SERVINGS.

Bananas Foster

3	TABLESPOONS LIGHTLY SALTED BUTTER
½	CUP PACKED DARK BROWN SUGAR
¼	CUP PINEAPPLE JUICE
1	TEASPOON FRESH LEMON JUICE
½	TEASPOON GROUND CINNAMON
¼	CUP DARK RUM
2	TABLESPOONS BANANA LIQUEUR
4	RIPE BANANAS, SPLIT LENGTHWISE IN THIRDS, THEN CROSSWISE IN HALF
4	CUPS (1 QUART) VANILLA ICE CREAM

IN A LARGE heavy saucepan over medium heat, stir butter and brown sugar until the butter is melted. Add pineapple juice, lemon juice and cinnamon. Cook, stirring, until bubbling, about 1 minute. Add rum and banana liqueur. Shake the pan until the mixture flames. When the flames extinguish, add bananas and sauté until tender, about 1 minute.

Scoop ice cream into 4 chilled dessert dishes and top with the banana mixture.

MAKES 4 SERVINGS.

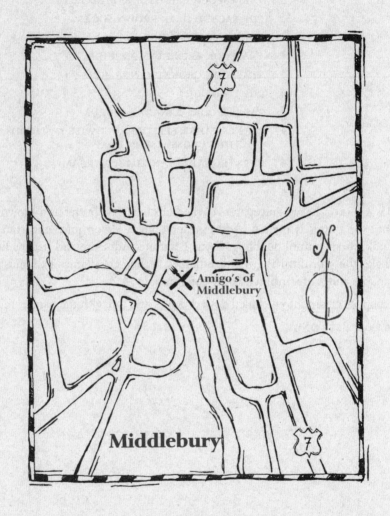

Amigo's of
Middlebury

Middlebury

Amigo's of Middlebury

4 Merchants Row
Middlebury, Vermont 05753
(802) 388-3624

AMIGO'S is located in the heart of Middlebury, across from the Village Green. This lively, casual restaurant serves reasonably priced authentic Mexican fare in one of two colorful dining rooms, and there is often live entertainment on weekends. The following recipes are a few of the house and customer favorites.

NEARBY & NOTEWORTHY: Stroll around quaint downtown Middlebury. Visit the nearby Vermont Book Shop or Otter Creek Books to browse, and peer over the bridge on Main Street at the falls below.

Tinga Poblano Burritos

Pico–de–Gallo

Black Beans

Sweet Chimichangas

Tinga Poblano Burritos

2½ POUNDS BONELESS PORK SHOULDER OR LEG,
    CUT INTO 1-INCH CUBES

½   POUND CHORIZO OR OTHER SPICY SAUSAGE,
    CASING REMOVED AND CRUMBLED

1   POUND POTATOES, CUBED

3   TOMATOES, CHOPPED

3   TABLESPOONS FINELY CHOPPED SPANISH ONIONS

3   CLOVES GARLIC, FINELY CHOPPED

1   CANNED CHIPOTLE PEPPER, SEEDED AND
    FINELY CHOPPED

8   8-INCH FLOUR TORTILLAS

¼   POUND MONTEREY JACK CHEESE, GRATED (1 CUP)

IN A LARGE heavy skillet, cook pork over medium-high heat until browned on all sides. Add chorizo, potatoes, tomatoes, onions, garlic and chipotles. Simmer for 1 hour, stirring occasionally.

Preheat oven to 350 degrees F.

Divide the pork mixture evenly among tortillas and sprinkle with ¾ cup of the Monterey Jack. Roll each tortilla around the filling and place seam-side down in a baking dish. Sprinkle the remaining ¼ cup Monterey Jack over the burritos and bake until the cheese is melted, about 3 minutes.

Serve the burritos with lettuce and pico-de-gallo.

MAKES 8 SERVINGS.

Pico–de–Gallo

For a spicier flavor, do not seed the jalapeño peppers
when preparing this condiment.

¼	TEASPOON DRIED OREGANO
4	TOMATOES, CHOPPED
3	TABLESPOONS FINELY CHOPPED SPANISH ONIONS
3	FRESH JALAPEÑO PEPPERS, SEEDED, IF DESIRED, AND FINELY CHOPPED
2	TABLESPOONS CHOPPED FRESH CILANTRO
	JUICE OF ½ LEMON
½	TEASPOON SALT

PREHEAT broiler.

Spread oregano in a small baking dish and broil until the oregano begins to smoke.

Combine tomatoes, onions, jalapeños and cilantro. Stir in the oregano, lemon juice and salt. Chill the pico-de-gallo for at least 1 hour before serving.

MAKES 8 SERVINGS.

Black Beans

1½   CUPS DRIED BLACK BEANS, SOAKED IN COLD WATER
        FOR AT LEAST 8 HOURS, DRAINED AND RINSED
3   TABLESPOONS CHOPPED SPANISH ONIONS
3   TEASPOONS ANCHO CHILI POWDER OR OTHER
        CHILI POWDER TO TASTE
½   TEASPOON GROUND CUMIN
½   TEASPOON GROUND BLACK PEPPER
½   TEASPOON GROUND RED PEPPER
       PINCH OF SALT

IN A LARGE pot, combine beans, onions, chili powder, cumin, black pepper, red pepper and salt. Add enough water to cover. Bring to a boil. Reduce heat and simmer, stirring occasionally, for 2 hours. (Most of the liquid should be absorbed.)

Remove the beans from the heat and mash.

MAKES 8 SERVINGS.

Sweet Chimichangas

1½	PINTS STRAWBERRIES, HULLED AND SLICED
2	LARGE APPLES, PEELED, CORED AND CHOPPED
2	BANANAS, SLICED
½	CUP SUGAR
2	TABLESPOONS APRICOT BRANDY
2	TEASPOONS PACKED LIGHT BROWN SUGAR
¼	TEASPOON GROUND NUTMEG PLUS ADDITIONAL FOR GARNISH
¼	TEASPOON GROUND CINNAMON
8	10-INCH FLOUR TORTILLAS
	VEGETABLE OIL FOR DEEP-FRYING
2	CUPS (1 PINT) VANILLA ICE CREAM

COMBINE strawberries, apples, bananas, sugar, brandy, brown sugar, nutmeg and cinnamon. Distribute the mixture evenly among tortillas and fold each into a tight square.

Pour enough oil to cover the tortillas into a large, deep heavy saucepan or deep-fryer. Heat until the oil registers 350 degrees F on a deep-frying thermometer. Fry for 30 seconds, in batches if necessary. (Do not turn the tortillas over as they may break apart.) Drain on paper towels.

Top the chimichangas with vanilla ice cream and sprinkle with nutmeg.

MAKES 8 SERVINGS.

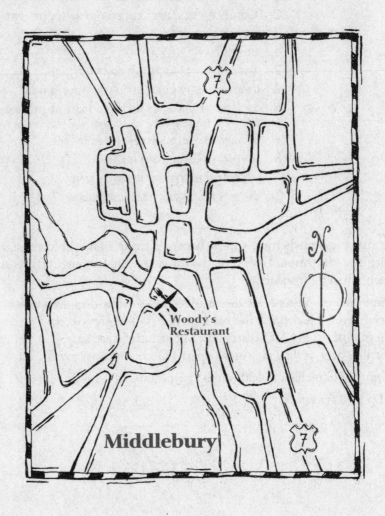

Woody's
Restaurant

Middlebury

7

7

Woody's Restaurant

5 Bakery Lane
Middlebury, Vermont 05753
(802) 388-4182

LOCATED ON THE BANKS of Otter Creek, and very close to the falls, Woody's Restaurant is a local favorite where you can count on innovative fare. The menu changes frequently according to seasonal availability of ingredients, and local products are used whenever possible. The unique deco-inspired interior has stunning views of the creek through the dining room's three-story glass wall.

NEARBY & NOTEWORTHY: Climb the hill from Woody's and head down the other side into Frog Hollow. Here, you will find the Vermont State Craft Center and other shops banked along the steep grade that descends to the foot of Otter Creek Falls. Traverse the footbridge that crosses the creek and visit the Historic Marble Works. Until the mid-1930s, marble blocks from nearby quarries were processed in this collection of white marble buildings. The building complex now houses shops and offices. Visit Danforth Pewterers, where you can purchase pewter lamps, bowls, vases, candlesticks, jewelry and other pewter items that are handcrafted nearby.

Cream of Butternut Squash Soup

Broccoli & Cheddar Fritters

Grilled Shrimp with Black Bean & Rice Salad

Chocolate Cheesecake

Cream of Butternut Squash Soup

Prepare this soup a day in advance to allow the flavors to intensify.

1	CUP DRY WHITE WINE
3	TABLESPOONS PURE MAPLE SYRUP
1	TABLESPOON TAMARI
⅛	TEASPOON GROUND NUTMEG
	PINCH OF GROUND CINNAMON
	SCANT PINCH OF GROUND CLOVES
	GROUND WHITE PEPPER
1	TABLESPOON LIGHTLY SALTED BUTTER
1	SMALL ONION, CHOPPED
1	BUTTERNUT SQUASH, PEELED AND CUBED
1	LARGE SWEET POTATO, PEELED AND CUBED
1	SMALL POTATO, PEELED AND CUBED
2	TEASPOONS SALT PLUS MORE TO TASTE
2	TART APPLES
	JUICE OF 1 LEMON
1	CUP HEAVY OR LIGHT CREAM

COMBINE wine, maple syrup, tamari, nutmeg, cinnamon, cloves and pepper to taste in a small saucepan. Simmer until reduced to one-third cup.

Meanwhile, melt butter in a large pot. Add onions, cover and cook over low heat until softened but not browned, 8 to 10 minutes. Stir in squash, sweet potatoes, potatoes and salt. Add enough water to cover by 2 inches. Bring to a boil. Reduce heat and simmer until the vegetables are very soft, about 30 minutes.

Puree the soup in a food processor or blender, in batches if necessary. Return to the pot and whisk in the reduced wine mixture. Bring to a simmer, stirring frequently, over low heat. While the soup is simmering, peel and finely chop apples; toss with lemon juice.

Meanwhile, heat cream almost to a boil. Whisk into the soup. For a thinner soup, whisk in water until the desired consistency is achieved. Season with salt and pepper to taste.

Ladle the soup into bowls and garnish with the chopped apples.

MAKES 6 SERVINGS.

Broccoli & Cheddar Fritters

1	CUP CHOPPED BROCCOLI
¾	CUP ALL-PURPOSE FLOUR
1	TEASPOON BAKING POWDER
¼	TEASPOON SALT
1	EGG
⅓	CUP MILK
¼	TEASPOON WORCESTERSHIRE SAUCE
¼	POUND CHEDDAR CHEESE, GRATED (1 CUP)
1	TABLESPOON LIGHTLY SALTED BUTTER
1	TABLESPOON VEGETABLE OIL

PREHEAT oven to 375 degrees F.

Boil broccoli in salted water to cover until just tender, 2 to 3 minutes. Plunge into cold water and pat dry.

Sift together flour, baking powder and salt. Whisk together egg, milk and Worcestershire. Add to the flour mixture and stir until well combined. Fold in the broccoli and Cheddar.

Heat butter and oil in a large heavy skillet over medium heat until the butter is melted and the moisture is evaporated. Use an ice cream scoop to scoop the batter into the skillet. Sauté two fritters at a time until golden brown, about 1 minute each side. Remove the fritters to a baking sheet. Repeat with the remaining batter. Bake the fritters until puffed, 6 to 8 minutes.

MAKES 12 FRITTERS.

Grilled Shrimp with Black Bean & Rice Salad

½	CUP OLIVE OIL
5	CLOVES GARLIC, FINELY CHOPPED
1	FRESH JALAPEÑO PEPPER, FINELY CHOPPED
1	TABLESPOON CHOPPED CILANTRO
1½	TEASPOONS FINELY CHOPPED FRESH GINGER
1	TEASPOON SALT
¼	TEASPOON CUMIN
¼	TEASPOON CHILI POWDER
	GRATED ZEST OF 1 LIME
	JUICE OF 2 LIMES
	JUICE OF 1 LEMON
	FRESHLY GROUND BLACK PEPPER
2	CUPS COOKED BLACK BEANS, RINSED AND DRAINED
2	CUPS COOKED BROWN RICE
1	CUP COOKED LONG-GRAIN WILD RICE
2	PLUM TOMATOES, CHOPPED
1	GREEN BELL PEPPER, CHOPPED
1	RED BELL PEPPER, CHOPPED
1	SPANISH ONION, CHOPPED
¼	CUP CHOPPED FRESH PARSLEY
3	POUNDS JUMBO SHRIMP, PEELED AND DEVEINED

Prepare a grill.

Whisk together oil, garlic, jalapeños, cilantro, ginger, salt, cumin, chili powder, lime zest, lime juice and lemon juice. Season with pepper to taste.

Combine beans, brown rice, wild rice, tomatoes, bell peppers, onions and parsley. Toss with two-thirds of the vinaigrette.

Place shrimp in a baking dish and toss with the remaining vinaigrette. Grill shrimp, covered, for 3 to 4 minutes on one side. Uncover, flip and grill for 2 minutes more.

Divide the bean salad equally among 6 plates. Arrange the shrimp on top. Serve with steamed sugar snap peas or broccoli.

Makes 6 servings.

Chocolate Cheesecake

*Woody prepares this with a homemade shortbread crust, but a
graham cracker crust will simplify preparation.*

CRUST

1	BOX (1 POUND) GRAHAM CRACKERS
6	TABLESPOONS BUTTER, MELTED
½	TEASPOON PURE VANILLA EXTRACT

FILLING

1½	POUNDS (THREE 8-OUNCE PACKAGES) CREAM CHEESE, AT ROOM TEMPERATURE
1	CUP SUGAR
12	OUNCES SEMISWEET CHOCOLATE CHIPS
¼	CUP HEAVY CREAM
4	EGGS, AT ROOM TEMPERATURE
1	TABLESPOON PURE VANILLA EXTRACT

To PREPARE CRUST: Preheat oven to 350 degrees F. Butter and flour a 9-inch springform pan; wrap with aluminum foil to seal and refrigerate until use.

Puree graham crackers. Blend the graham cracker crumbs, melted butter and vanilla until well combined. Press into the bottom of the prepared springform pan. Bake the crust until lightly golden, 8 to 10 minutes. Remove from the oven and reduce heat to 275 degrees F.

TO PREPARE FILLING: Blend cream cheese and ½ cup of the sugar until smooth, scraping the sides of the bowl frequently. Whisk vigorously to lighten.

In a double boiler over medium heat, heat chocolate chips and cream until the chocolate is melted and the mixture is smooth. Add to the cream cheese mixture and whisk until smooth.

Beat eggs with the remaining ½ cup sugar and vanilla until the eggs are pale and begin to cling to the whisk. Fold into the cream cheese mixture until well blended.

Pour ½ inch of hot water into a roasting pan. Scrape the batter into the prepared springform pan and set in the roasting pan. Bake the cheesecake until the filling resembles well-set gelatin, 1 to 1½ hours. Let cool in the oven with the door ajar for 30 minutes. Refrigerate for at least 4 hours before serving.

MAKES ONE 9-INCH CHEESECAKE.

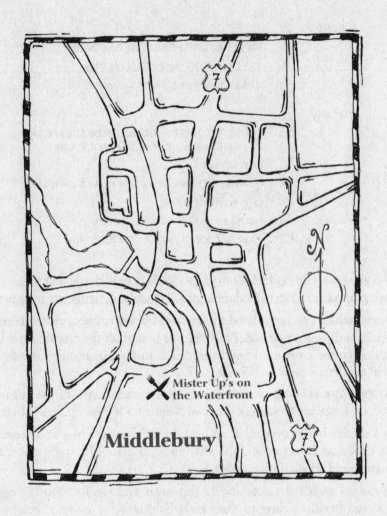

✕ **Mister Up's on
the Waterfront**

Middlebury

Mister Up's on the Waterfront

Bakery Lane
Middlebury, Vermont 05753
(802) 388-6724

THE WATERFRONT at Mister Up's is Otter Creek, one of the state's longest rivers and, as rarely happens, a river flowing north. The riverside deck draws crowds in the summer; the extensive menu and casual atmosphere are enjoyed by guests year-round. Although patrons have not recently reported the otters for which the creek was named, muskrats have been seen making their way downstream. Owner Marty is often at the door to greet you and to make sure your visit is enjoyable.

NEARBY & NOTEWORTHY: Middlebury College, one of the nation's leading small liberal arts colleges, is an easy walk from Mister Up's. Pick up a campus map at the Admissions Office to guide you on your tour. Be sure to visit Painter Hall, one of the three native Vermont limestone buildings that make up "old stone row." It is the oldest college building in the state still in use. Also explore the Middlebury College Museum of Art, which has an excellent permanent collection and temporary exhibits, and check the event schedule for the Center for the Arts, which hosts concerts, plays and dance performances.

Stellar Salad

Dirty Steak with Sweet Horseradish Sauce

Mud Pie

Stellar Salad

*This salad is best when the vegetables are grilled over mesquite chips,
but you can grill them conventionally.*

VINAIGRETTE

½	CUP DIJON MUSTARD
⅓	CUP RED WINE VINEGAR
3	EGGS
1	CLOVE GARLIC, FINELY CHOPPED
1	TEASPOON DRIED MINCED ONION
1	TEASPOON DRIED MARJORAM
1	TEASPOON DRIED BASIL
1	TEASPOON DRIED THYME LEAVES
1	TEASPOON DRIED TARRAGON
1	CUP EXTRA-VIRGIN OLIVE OIL

VEGETABLE SALAD

2	CARROTS, PEELED AND CUT LENGTHWISE IN THIRDS
1	RED BELL PEPPER, CORED, SEEDED AND CUT IN HALF
1	GREEN BELL PEPPER, CORED, SEEDED AND CUT IN HALF
3	SMALL ZUCCHINI, CUT LENGTHWISE IN THIRDS
2	SMALL YELLOW SQUASH, CUT LENGTHWISE IN THIRDS
1	EGGPLANT (1 POUND), PEELED AND CUT INTO ¼-INCH-THICK SLICES
6	SCALLIONS
4	FRESH SHIITAKE MUSHROOMS, TRIMMED
¼	POUND GOAT CHEESE, CRUMBLED (1 CUP)
1	CUP WALNUT HALVES
8	CUPS WASHED, DRIED AND TORN ROMAINE LETTUCE

To prepare vinaigrette: Puree mustard, vinegar, 2 tablespoons water, eggs, garlic, dried onion, marjoram, basil, thyme and tarragon in a blender or food processor. With the motor running, slowly add oil and blend until smooth.

TO PREPARE VEGETABLE SALAD: Prepare a grill.

Grill vegetables until just tender, in batches if necessary. Carrots will take about 5 minutes each side, bell peppers about 5 minutes (grill skin-side down and do not turn over), zucchini, yellow squash and eggplant 2 to 3 minutes each side and scallions and shiitakes 2 to 3 minutes (do not turn over). Let cool completely.

Preheat oven to 400 degrees F.

Cut the vegetables into julienne, toss together and arrange in four piles on a baking sheet. Distribute goat cheese and walnut halves evenly on top of the piles and sprinkle with the dressing. Bake until the goat cheese is browned around the edges, 10 to 15 minutes.

Arrange romaine on 4 plates and top with the vegetable mixture.

MAKES 4 SERVINGS.

Dirty Steak with Sweet Horseradish Sauce

*Traditionally this steak is first seared by throwing it
on the hot coals. Hence, its name.*

DIRTY STEAK

2	CUPS PURE MAPLE SYRUP
2	CUPS HONEY
2	CUPS WHOLE-GRAIN MUSTARD
¾	CUP WHISKEY
6	SCALLIONS, SLICED DIAGONALLY
2	CLOVES GARLIC, CHOPPED
4	12-OUNCE STRIP STEAKS

HORSERADISH SAUCE

4	SCALLIONS, WHITE PART ONLY, SLICED DIAGONALLY
½	CUP SOUR CREAM
2	TABLESPOONS MAYONNAISE
1	TABLESPOON HONEY
1	TABLESPOON BOTTLED HORSERADISH, DRAINED
	GRATED ZEST OF 1 LEMON
	JUICE OF ½ LEMON
1½	TEASPOONS CHOPPED FRESH PARSLEY

TO PREPARE DIRTY STEAK: Whisk together maple syrup, honey, mustard, 1 cup water and whiskey. Stir in scallions and garlic. Marinate steaks in the maple syrup mixture for 24 hours. A few hours before you plan to grill the steaks, prepare the horseradish sauce.

TO PREPARE HORSERADISH SAUCE: Combine all ingredients and let stand for 1 to 2 hours before serving.

TO GRILL DIRTY STEAK: Prepare a grill.

Grill the steaks for about 7 minutes each side for medium-rare. Serve with baked potatoes, sautéed zucchini and the horseradish sauce.

MAKES 4 SERVINGS.

Mud Pie

PIE

½	GALLON COFFEE ICE CREAM
1	PACKAGE (1 POUND) OREO COOKIES
2	TABLESPOONS LIGHTLY SALTED BUTTER, AT ROOM TEMPERATURE

TOPPING

¼	POUND (1 STICK) LIGHTLY SALTED BUTTER
4½	OUNCES (4½ SQUARES) UNSWEETENED CHOCOLATE
1	CUP SUGAR
¾	CUP HEAVY CREAM
¾	TEASPOON PURE VANILLA EXTRACT

To PREPARE PIE: Soften ice cream by letting it stand at room temperature for 10 to 20 minutes.

Meanwhile, gently twist apart cookies and scrape out and discard the white filling. Puree the chocolate wafers. Cream the cookie crumbs and butter. Press the mixture into a 9-inch pie pan, making sure the piecrust reaches the rim of the pan.

Mound the softened ice cream in the piecrust and smooth the top. Cover and freeze until firm, at least 4 hours. Make the topping while the pie is freezing.

TO PREPARE TOPPING: In a heavy saucepan over medium heat, melt butter and chocolate. Gradually add sugar and whisk until it is dissolved. Let cool.

Stir cream and vanilla into the chocolate mixture. Spread the topping over the pie and freeze until firm, about 2 hours.

MAKES ONE 9-INCH PIE.

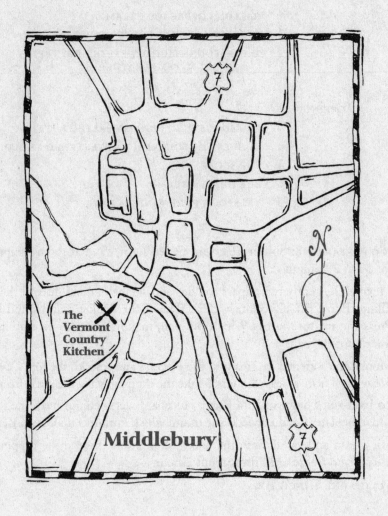

The
Vermont
Country
Kitchen

Middlebury

7

7

N

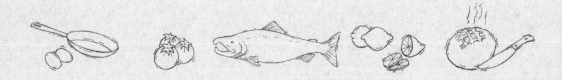

The Vermont Country Kitchen

3 Park Street
Middlebury, Vermont 05753
(802) 388-8646

THE VERMONT COUNTRY KITCHEN is a gourmet specialty food store and café that serves homemade baked goods and soups as well as unique rolled sandwiches. A full selection of kitchen gadgets, cookware and wine is also offered for sale. It is the perfect place to stock up for an impromptu picnic, and the staff specializes in creating gift baskets to take home with you or to give to family and friends.

NEARBY & NOTEWORTHY: The Sheldon Museum, just a few doors away, was once the home of Henry Sheldon, a great collector of artifacts used in everyday life in the late 1800s. With his collection now on display, the museum gives a sense of how life was lived at the turn of the century. The museum's Cerf Gallery has a changing schedule of exhibits.

French Breakfast Muffins

Carrot Pecan Muffins

Hungarian Mushroom Soup

Walnut Chocolate Chip Scones

French Breakfast Muffins

MUFFINS

2	EGGS
¾	CUP MILK
2½	CUPS ALL-PURPOSE FLOUR
1¼	CUPS SUGAR
1	TABLESPOON BAKING POWDER
1½	TEASPOONS GROUND NUTMEG
½	TEASPOON SALT
¼	POUND (1 STICK) LIGHTLY SALTED BUTTER OR MARGARINE, MELTED

TOPPING

¾	CUP SUGAR
1½	TEASPOONS GROUND CINNAMON
½	TEASPOON PURE VANILLA EXTRACT
12	TABLESPOONS (1½ STICKS) LIGHTLY SALTED BUTTER OR MARGARINE, MELTED

TO PREPARE MUFFINS: Preheat oven to 400 degrees F. Lightly grease a 12-cup muffin tin.

Beat eggs and milk in a large bowl until well combined. Sift together flour, sugar, baking powder, nutmeg and salt. Add to the egg mixture and stir until just combined. Stir in melted butter or margarine.

Divide the batter evenly among the prepared muffin cups. Bake the muffins until golden brown and a tester comes out clean, 17 to 20 minutes. Make the topping while the muffins are cooling.

TO PREPARE TOPPING: Combine sugar, cinnamon and vanilla in a small bowl.

Brush the warm muffins with melted butter or margarine and roll in the sugar mixture.

MAKES 12 MUFFINS.

Carrot Pecan Muffins

2	CUPS ALL-PURPOSE FLOUR
1¼	CUPS SUGAR
2	TEASPOONS BAKING SODA
2	TEASPOONS GROUND CINNAMON
½	TEASPOON SALT
	DASH OF MACE
2	CUPS GRATED CARROTS (ABOUT 4 CARROTS)
1	APPLE, PEELED, CORED AND GRATED
½	CUP RAISINS
½	CUP CHOPPED PECANS
½	CUP SWEETENED SHREDDED COCONUT
3	EGGS
1	CUP VEGETABLE OIL
2	TEASPOONS PURE VANILLA EXTRACT

PREHEAT oven to 350 degrees F. Lightly grease 18 muffin cups in two 12-cup tins.

Sift flour, sugar, baking soda, cinnamon, salt and mace into a large bowl. Stir in carrots, apples, raisins, pecans and coconut. Beat eggs, oil and vanilla until well combined. Add to the flour mixture and mix well.

Divide the batter evenly among the 18 prepared muffin cups. Fill the empty cups with water. Bake the muffins until the tops spring back when lightly touched, 30 to 35 minutes.

MAKES 18 MUFFINS.

Hungarian Mushroom Soup

4	TABLESPOONS LIGHTLY SALTED BUTTER
2	LARGE ONIONS, CHOPPED
1	TEASPOON SALT
¾	POUND MUSHROOMS, TRIMMED AND SLICED
2	CUPS BEEF STOCK, PREFERABLY HOMEMADE
1	TABLESPOON TAMARI
1	TABLESPOON HUNGARIAN PAPRIKA (AVAILABLE AT SPECIALTY FOOD SHOPS)
2	TEASPOONS CHOPPED FRESH DILL
3	TABLESPOONS ALL-PURPOSE FLOUR
1	CUP MILK
½	CUP SOUR CREAM
2	TEASPOONS FRESH LEMON JUICE
	SALT & FRESHLY GROUND BLACK PEPPER
¼	CUP CHOPPED FRESH PARSLEY

MELT 2 tablespoons of the butter in a skillet. Add onions and salt and sauté until the onions are translucent, about 3 minutes. Add mushrooms, ½ cup of the beef stock, tamari, paprika and 1 teaspoon of the dill. Cover and simmer for 15 minutes.

Meanwhile, melt the remaining 2 tablespoons butter in a large pot. Whisk in flour and cook over low heat, whisking constantly until smooth. Add milk and simmer, stirring constantly, until thickened, about 10 minutes. Stir in the mushroom mixture and the remaining 1½ cups beef stock. Cover and simmer for 10 to 15 minutes more.

Just before serving, stir sour cream and lemon juice into the soup. Season with salt and pepper to taste. Garnish with the remaining 1 teaspoon dill and parsley.

MAKES 4 SERVINGS.

Walnut Chocolate Chip Scones

2	CUPS ALL-PURPOSE FLOUR
⅓	CUP PACKED DARK BROWN SUGAR
1½	TEASPOONS BAKING POWDER
½	TEASPOON BAKING SODA
¼	TEASPOON SALT
6	TABLESPOONS UNSALTED BUTTER, CUT INTO BITS
1	EGG
½	CUP BUTTERMILK
1½	TEASPOONS PURE VANILLA EXTRACT
6	OUNCES SEMISWEET CHOCOLATE CHIPS
½	CUP CHOPPED WALNUTS PLUS ADDITIONAL FOR GARNISH

PREHEAT oven to 400 degrees F. Lightly butter a 9-inch pie pan.

Stir together flour, brown sugar, baking powder, baking soda and salt. Distribute butter over the flour mixture and blend until the mixture resembles coarse meal. Beat egg, buttermilk and vanilla until well combined. Add to the flour mixture and mix well. Fold in chocolate chips and walnuts. (The dough will be sticky.)

Form the dough into an 8-inch circle in the prepared pie pan. Arrange additional walnuts around the edge of the dough. Cut into 8 wedges with a serrated knife. Bake the scones until golden brown and a tester comes out clean, 17 to 19 minutes.

MAKES 8 SCONES.

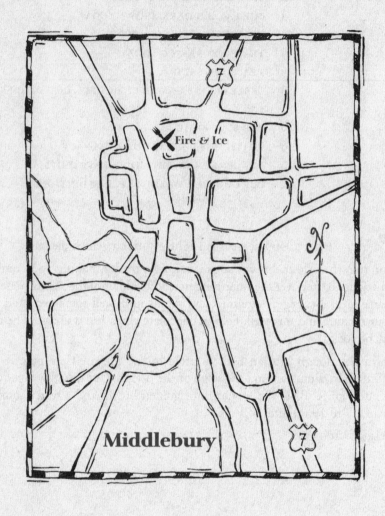

Fire & Ice

Middlebury

Fire & Ice

26 Seymour Street
Middlebury, Vermont 05753
(802) 388-7166/(800) 367-7166

FIRE & ICE opened in 1974, just a few blocks from downtown Middlebury. This destination dinner house specializes in steak and seafood as well as the house favorites featured below. The eclectic decor is unique and worthy of special attention—regional photos and Middlebury College memorabilia as well as sporting equipment and musical instruments decorate the interior. Host and owner Dale, one of the numerous Middlebury College graduates who stayed on in the community, is often at the door to greet you.

NEARBY & NOTEWORTHY: Just a short distance away you'll find Vermont artist Woody Jackson's Holy Cow Store, featuring his artwork and other cow gift items. This artist has memorialized the Holstein cow as the heroine of Vermont.

Stuffed Mushroom Caps

Potage Crecy

Champagne Chicken

Frozen Peanut Pie with Chocolate Sauce

Stuffed Mushroom Caps

¼	POUND (1 STICK) LIGHTLY SALTED BUTTER
3	CELERY STALKS, CHOPPED
1	ONION, CHOPPED
1	CUP GRATED CARROTS (ABOUT 2 CARROTS)
3	CLOVES GARLIC, FINELY CHOPPED
¼	CUP DRY WHITE WINE
1	BAG (10 OUNCES) FRESH SPINACH, COOKED UNTIL WILTED, CHOPPED
⅓	CUP GRATED PARMESAN CHEESE
⅓	CUP CHOPPED WALNUTS
3	TABLESPOONS CHOPPED FRESH PARSLEY
1	TEASPOON SALT
½	TEASPOON DRIED THYME LEAVES
½	TEASPOON GROUND BLACK PEPPER
1	CUP DRY SEASONED BREADCRUMBS
32	MUSHROOMS, STEMS REMOVED
¼	POUND CHEDDAR CHEESE, GRATED (1 CUP)

PREHEAT oven to 400 degrees F. Lightly oil a baking sheet.

Melt butter in a large skillet. Stir in celery and onions and cook until softened, about 10 minutes. Add carrots, garlic and wine. Cook, stirring, for 5 minutes more. Remove from the heat. Stir in spinach, Parmesan, walnuts, parsley, salt, thyme and pepper. Add breadcrumbs and mix well.

Arrange mushroom caps on the prepared baking sheet. Fill each cavity with the spinach mixture and sprinkle with Cheddar. Bake the mushrooms until the Cheddar is browned and bubbly, 15 to 20 minutes.

MAKES 8 SERVINGS.

Potage Crecy

6   CARROTS, PEELED AND CHOPPED

6   POTATOES, PEELED AND CUBED

1   ONION, CHOPPED

2   CUBES CHICKEN BOUILLON

4   TABLESPOONS LIGHTLY SALTED BUTTER

½   CUP SOUR CREAM

    MILK FOR THINNING SOUP (OPTIONAL)

    SALT & GROUND BLACK PEPPER

IN A LARGE pot, cover carrots, potatoes and onions with cold water. Add bouillon cubes and boil until the vegetables are tender, about 25 minutes. Remove from the heat and stir in butter and sour cream.

Puree the soup in a food processor or blender, in batches if necessary. For a thinner soup, whisk in milk until the desired consistency is achieved. Season with salt and pepper to taste.

MAKES 8 SERVINGS.

Champagne Chicken

¼   CUP OLIVE OIL
4   BONELESS, SKINLESS CHICKEN BREASTS,
    CUT IN HALF AND POUNDED
1   CUP CHOPPED MUSHROOMS
4   CUPS HEAVY CREAM
½   CUP CHAMPAGNE OR DRY WHITE WINE

HEAT oil in a large skillet over medium-high heat. Add chicken and sauté until white, not pink, about 10 minutes. Remove to a plate and keep warm by loosely covering with aluminum foil.

Add mushrooms, cream and Champagne or wine to the skillet. Cook until the sauce is reduced by one-half. Spoon the sauce over the chicken and serve with rice and steamed vegetables.

MAKES 8 SERVINGS.

Frozen Peanut Pie
with Chocolate Sauce

PEANUT PIE

1	CUP HEAVY CREAM
½	POUND (ONE 8-OUNCE PACKAGE) CREAM CHEESE, AT ROOM TEMPERATURE
1	CUP CONFECTIONERS' SUGAR
½	CUP CREAMY PEANUT BUTTER
1	PREPARED GRAHAM CRACKER PIECRUST
½	CUP CHOPPED ROASTED PEANUTS

CHOCOLATE SAUCE

4	OUNCES SWEET CHOCOLATE, FINELY CHOPPED
2	OUNCES (2 SQUARES) UNSWEETENED CHOCOLATE, FINELY CHOPPED
1	CUP SUGAR
1	CUP LIGHT CORN SYRUP
¾	CUP HALF-AND-HALF
2	TEASPOONS PURE VANILLA EXTRACT
	PINCH OF SALT

TO MAKE PEANUT PIE: Whip cream until soft peaks begin to form.

In another bowl, whip cream cheese until fluffy. Add confectioners' sugar and peanut butter and beat until well blended. Fold in the whipped cream.

Scrape the cream cheese mixture into piecrust. Top with peanuts and freeze until firm, at least 4 hours.

TO MAKE CHOCOLATE SAUCE: In a double boiler over low heat, whisk sweet chocolate, unsweetened chocolate, sugar and corn syrup until the chocolate is melted and the mixture is smooth. Remove from the heat and whisk in half-and-half, vanilla and salt.

Serve the pie topped with the hot chocolate sauce and whipped cream.

MAKES ONE 8- OR 9-INCH PIE.

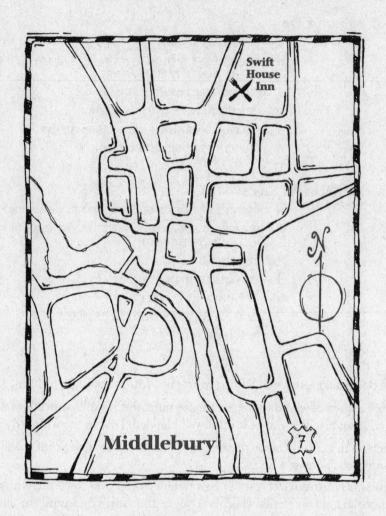

Swift
House
Inn

Middlebury

7

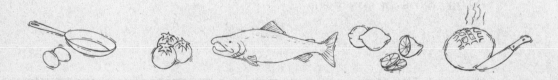

Swift House Inn

25 Stewart Lane
Middlebury, Vermont 05753
(802) 388-9925

S WIFT HOUSE INN is beautifully situated at the crest of a large sloping
lawn amidst three acres of landscaped grounds. Located just two blocks
north of the center of town, this elegant 1815 estate was once the home of
the Stewarts, a prominent family who were longtime residents of
Middlebury. Seasonal and regional fare is served in the intimate candlelit
dining room, and guests may choose wines from a Wine Spectator award-
winning list.

NEARBY & NOTEWORTHY: Follow Seymour Street to the 1805 covered
bridge, an outstanding example of a two-lane covered bridge. After passing
through, bear right to reach the University of Vermont Morgan Horse
Farm—a picturesque working farm that has been in operation since the
1870s.

Fresh Fennel & Roasted Garlic Soup

Warm Shrimp Caesar Salad with Three Relishes

Herb–Crusted Filet Mignon with Drambuie Demi–Glace

Bourbon Carrots

Double Chocolate Terrine

Fresh Fennel &
Roasted Garlic Soup

8	CLOVES GARLIC, PEELED
¼	CUP VEGETABLE OIL
12	CUPS CHICKEN STOCK, PREFERABLY HOMEMADE
1	ONION, CHOPPED
1	FENNEL BULB, CHOPPED
1	TABLESPOON FRESH THYME OR 1 TEASPOON DRIED THYME LEAVES
3	BAY LEAVES
2	CUPS HEAVY CREAM
	GROUND RED PEPPER
	SALT & GROUND BLACK PEPPER

IN A LARGE pot, sauté garlic in oil over low heat until fragrant but not browned. Stir in chicken stock, onions, fennel, thyme and bay leaves. Simmer until the fennel is very tender, about 45 minutes. (The stock should reduce by almost one-half.)

Discard the bay leaves. Puree the soup in a food processor or blender, in batches if necessary. Stir in cream and season with red pepper, salt and black pepper to taste.

MAKES 4 SERVINGS.

Warm Shrimp Caesar Salad with Three Relishes

Sun-Dried Tomato Relish

4	SUN-DRIED TOMATOES, FINELY CHOPPED
2	TABLESPOONS CHOPPED FRESH HERBS (TARRAGON, BASIL, OREGANO)
1	SHALLOT, FINELY CHOPPED
½	CLOVE GARLIC, FINELY CHOPPED
5	TABLESPOONS OLIVE OIL
3	TABLESPOONS RED WINE VINEGAR

Three-Onion Relish

1	SMALL SPANISH ONION, THINLY SLICED
1	SMALL RED ONION, THINLY SLICED
1	TABLESPOON SNIPPED FRESH CHIVES
1	TABLESPOON CAPERS
	GRATED ZEST OF 1 LEMON
	JUICE OF 1 LEMON
3	TABLESPOONS OLIVE OIL
1	TEASPOON HONEY

Black Olive Relish

15	NIÇOISE OLIVES, PITTED AND CUT INTO QUARTERS
1	SHALLOT, FINELY CHOPPED
1	TABLESPOON CHOPPED FRESH BASIL
1	TABLESPOON CHOPPED FRESH PARSLEY
1	TABLESPOON FRESHLY GROUND BLACK PEPPER
1	CLOVE GARLIC, FINELY CHOPPED
	PINCH OF SUGAR
3	TABLESPOONS OLIVE OIL
1	TABLESPOON BALSAMIC VINEGAR

DRESSING

¼	CUP GRATED PARMESAN CHEESE
3	CLOVES GARLIC
2	ANCHOVY FILLETS
1	EGG
	JUICE OF 1 LEMON
1	TABLESPOON WORCESTERSHIRE SAUCE
1	TABLESPOON WHITE WINE VINEGAR
1	TABLESPOON DIJON MUSTARD
1	CUP OLIVE OIL
	TABASCO SAUCE
	SALT & GROUND BLACK PEPPER

SALAD

2	TABLESPOONS OLIVE OIL
12	JUMBO SHRIMP, PEELED AND DEVEINED
2	TABLESPOONS DRY WHITE WINE
1	CLOVE GARLIC, FINELY CHOPPED
1	HEAD ROMAINE LETTUCE, OUTER LEAVES DISCARDED, REMAINING LEAVES WASHED, DRIED AND TORN INTO BITE-SIZE PIECES
¼	CUP GRATED PARMESAN CHEESE
1	CUP SEASONED CROUTONS, PREFERABLY HOMEMADE

TO PREPARE RELISHES: Combine sun-dried tomato relish ingredients. Mix well. Stir occasionally until serving. Repeat the procedure to prepare three-onion relish and black olive relish. If possible, prepare the relishes a day in advance to allow the flavors to intensify.

TO PREPARE DRESSING: Puree Parmesan, garlic, anchovies, egg, lemon juice, Worcestershire, vinegar and mustard in a food processor. With the motor running, pour in oil in a steady stream and process until smooth. Season with Tabasco, salt and pepper to taste.

TO PREPARE SALAD: Heat oil in a skillet over medium-high heat. Add shrimp and sauté until the shrimp begin to turn pink, about 2 minutes. Add wine and garlic and sauté for 2 minutes more.

Arrange romaine and the shrimp on 4 plates. Spoon a dollop of each relish onto the romaine. Drizzle the dressing over the salad and top with grated Parmesan and croutons.

MAKES 4 SERVINGS.

Herb–Crusted Filet Mignon with Drambuie Demi–Glace

4	6-OUNCE FILET MIGNONS
4	STRIPS COB-SMOKED BACON
2	TABLESPOONS GROUND WHITE PEPPER
2	TABLESPOONS CRACKED BLACK PEPPER
2	TABLESPOONS FENNEL SEEDS
2	TABLESPOONS DRIED THYME LEAVES
2	TABLESPOONS DRIED ROSEMARY
1	TABLESPOON SALT
1	SHALLOT, FINELY CHOPPED
¼	CUP DRY RED WINE
3	CUPS VEAL OR BEEF STOCK, PREFERABLY HOMEMADE
2	TABLESPOONS OLIVE OIL
¼	CUP DRAMBUIE
3	TABLESPOONS DRIED BLACK CURRANTS
2	TABLESPOONS UNSALTED BUTTER, CUT INTO BITS

WRAP each filet with a strip of bacon and secure with butcher's twine or a toothpick. Combine white pepper, black pepper, fennel, thyme, rosemary and salt in a small bowl. Dredge the filets with this mixture.

Preheat oven to 400 degrees F.

In a skillet, simmer shallots in wine until the liquid is almost completely evaporated. Add veal or beef stock and simmer until only 1½ cups of the liquid remains. Remove from the heat.

Heat oil in a large ovenproof skillet over high heat. When the skillet is very hot, sear the filets until browned on all sides. Transfer the skillet to the oven and bake the filets for 12 to 15 minutes for medium-rare. Remove to serving plates and loosely cover with aluminum foil to keep warm.

Return the shallot mixture to the heat and stir in Drambuie and currants. Whisk in butter until just melted.

Spoon the sauce over the filets and serve with rosemary and garlic roasted potatoes.

MAKES 4 SERVINGS.

Bourbon Carrots

4	CARROTS, PEELED AND THINLY SLICED
2	TABLESPOONS PACKED LIGHT BROWN SUGAR
2	TABLESPOONS UNSALTED BUTTER
	SALT & GROUND WHITE PEPPER
3	TABLESPOONS BOURBON

PLACE carrots in a small saucepan with ¼ cup water, brown sugar and butter. Season with salt and pepper to taste. Simmer until the carrots are tender and the liquid is evaporated. Add bourbon and simmer for 1 to 2 minutes more.

MAKES 4 SERVINGS.

Double Chocolate Terrine

A topping of fresh berries provides a refreshing contrast to the rich terrine.

1	CUP HEAVY CREAM
4	TABLESPOONS UNSALTED BUTTER
¼	CUP SUGAR
8	OUNCES BITTERSWEET CHOCOLATE, FINELY CHOPPED
¼	CUP CRÈME DE CACAO

LINE a loaf pan with plastic wrap.

In a heavy saucepan over medium-low heat, bring cream, butter and sugar to a rolling boil. Reduce heat to low and add chocolate. Whisk until the chocolate is melted and the mixture is smooth. Remove from the heat and let cool.

Stir in crème de cacao and pour the mixture into the prepared loaf pan. Refrigerate until solid, 4 to 6 hours.

When ready to serve, cut the terrine into thin slices.

MAKES 4 SERVINGS.

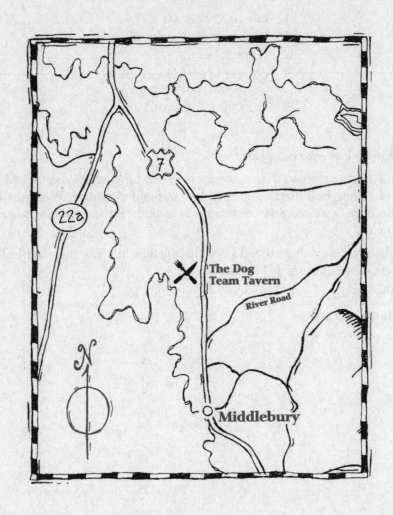

The Dog
Team Tavern

River Road

22a

7

N

Middlebury

The Dog Team Tavern

Dog Team Road
Middlebury, Vermont 05753
(802) 388-7651

THE DOG TEAM TAVERN, a landmark renowned for its hearty Vermont food and, especially, its sticky buns, has been serving the public for more than 50 years. Besides the food, one of the most interesting features about the Dog Team is its origin. It was built and operated as a tea house in the 1920s and 1930s by Lady Anne Grenfell, wife of the noted Labrador doctor and missionary Sir Wilfred Grenfell. The tea house sold handicrafts from Labrador and Newfoundland to raise money for those areas. Artifacts reminiscent of the philanthropic history of the tavern, such as a portrait of Sir Wilfred prominently displayed in the lobby, as well as pencil sketches depicting dog sleds and icebergs, are still in evidence.

NEARBY & NOTEWORTHY: Follow the scenic River Road to New Haven Mills on your way to the next stop (Mary's at Baldwin Creek). You will pass through some of the area's most productive farmland and along the banks of the New Haven River, an excellent fishing stream popular among local anglers.

Sticky Buns

Orange–Ginger Pork Chops

Butternut Squash

Maple Oatmeal Pie

Sticky Buns

¾   POUND POTATOES, PEELED AND CUBED

¼   POUND (1 STICK) MARGARINE, AT ROOM
       TEMPERATURE

2¾   CUPS SUGAR

1½   TEASPOONS SALT

1   PACKAGE ACTIVE DRY YEAST

2   EGGS, WELL BEATEN

7   CUPS ALL-PURPOSE FLOUR

1½   CUPS PACKED LIGHT BROWN SUGAR

1½   CUPS CHOPPED WALNUTS

½   POUND (2 STICKS) LIGHTLY SALTED BUTTER,
       MELTED

¼   CUP GROUND CINNAMON

Boil potatoes in salted water to cover until tender, about 10 minutes. Drain the potatoes, reserving 1½ cups of the cooking liquid, and mash. Measure 1 cup of the mashed potatoes and reserve the rest for another use.

Stir together the mashed potatoes, margarine, ½ cup of the sugar and salt. Cool to lukewarm and add yeast, eggs and the reserved 1½ cups cooking liquid. Mix well. Add flour and stir. Knead on a lightly floured surface until the dough is smooth and elastic. Set in a lightly oiled bowl, cover with a damp cloth and let rise in a warm place until doubled in bulk. Punch down and refrigerate until chilled, about 1 hour.

Butter three 9-inch round or square baking dishes. Distribute brown sugar evenly among the pans. Sprinkle with enough water to make the sugar very wet. Distribute walnuts evenly over the brown sugar.

Roll out the dough into a ½-inch-thick rectangle on a well-floured surface. Brush with melted butter. Stir together the remaining 2¼ cups sugar and cinnamon. Sprinkle over the buttered dough. Roll up the dough as you would a jelly roll. Cut into ½-inch-thick slices. Arrange the slices cut-side up in the prepared pans so that they are almost touching. Cover and let rise in a warm place until doubled in bulk, about 1 hour.

Preheat oven to 350 degrees F.

Bake the sticky buns until golden brown, 20 to 30 minutes. Immediately invert the buns onto a plate.

MAKES 6 TO 8 STICKY BUNS PER PAN.

Orange–Ginger Pork Chops

1   CAN (12 OUNCES) ORANGE JUICE
         CONCENTRATE, THAWED

¾   CUP LIGHT SOY SAUCE

1¼   TEASPOONS GROUND GINGER

¼   TEASPOON DRIED MINCED GARLIC

¼   TEASPOON GROUND WHITE PEPPER

8   PORK LOIN CHOPS, EACH ABOUT
         ½ INCH THICK

IN A LARGE pan, whisk together juice concentrate, 1½ cups water, soy sauce, ginger, dried garlic and pepper. Arrange pork chops in the pan and marinate in the refrigerator for 1 hour.

Preheat broiler.

Broil the chops for 4 to 5 minutes each side, or until the pork is no longer pink inside. Serve the pork chops with mashed potatoes and green beans.

MAKES 8 SERVINGS.

Butternut Squash

2   BUTTERNUT SQUASH (ABOUT 2 POUNDS EACH),
    PEELED AND CUBED
4   TABLESPOONS LIGHTLY SALTED BUTTER
¼   CUP PACKED DARK BROWN SUGAR
½   TEASPOON SALT
⅛   TEASPOON GROUND WHITE PEPPER

BOIL squash in salted water to cover until tender, about 20 minutes. Drain well. Mash the squash with butter, brown sugar, salt and pepper.

MAKES 8 SERVINGS.

Maple Oatmeal Pie

3	EGGS, LIGHTLY BEATEN
2	CUPS PURE GRADE B MAPLE SYRUP
3	TABLESPOONS LIGHTLY SALTED BUTTER, MELTED
1	TEASPOON PURE VANILLA EXTRACT
⅔	CUP UNSWEETENED SHREDDED COCONUT
⅔	CUP QUICK-COOKING ROLLED OATS
½	CUP CHOPPED WALNUTS
1	9-INCH UNBAKED PIECRUST

PREHEAT oven to 325 degrees F.

In a large bowl, beat eggs, maple syrup, melted butter and vanilla until well combined. Stir in coconut, oats and walnuts.

Pour the mixture into piecrust. Bake the pie until golden brown, about 45 minutes.

MAKES ONE 9-INCH PIE.

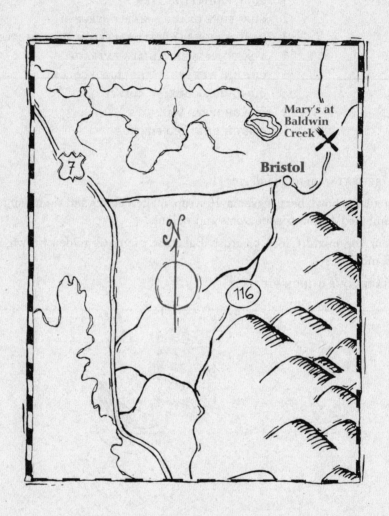

Mary's at
Baldwin
Creek

7

Bristol

N

116

Mary's at Baldwin Creek

Junction of Routes 116 and 17
P.O. Box 312
Bristol, Vermont 05443
(802) 453-2432

ESTABLISHED IN 1972 in downtown Bristol, Mary's now occupies a rambling farmhouse on the banks of Baldwin Creek. Innovative cuisine is served in one of the four countrified but elegant dining rooms, and there are five guest rooms for those who are seeking an overnight getaway or to escape for a longer sojourn. One of the barns on the property has been artfully converted into a retail store that sells specialty foods and eclectic housewares.

NEARBY & NOTEWORTHY: Bartlett Falls, a popular swimming hole, is just a short drive away on the road to Lincoln. Even if summer's heat is not pressing, pass the time by watching brilliantly colored leaves whirl their way through the series of pools and cascade over the rock ledges. In winter, the water freezes and forms arcs of snow-white and sea-blue ripples.

Dilled Tomato Bisque

Black Bread

New England Crab Cakes with Corn & Sweet Pepper Sauce

Grilled Venison with Red Wine & Gorgonzola Sauce

Salmon with Strawberry & Black Peppercorn Vinaigrette

Raspberry Gratin

Dilled Tomato Bisque

4	TABLESPOONS UNSALTED BUTTER
1	MEDIUM ONION, FINELY CHOPPED
2	CLOVES GARLIC, FINELY CHOPPED
1	TABLESPOON CHOPPED FRESH DILL
1	CAN (28 OUNCES) WHOLE PEELED TOMATOES, WITH JUICE
1	CUP COOKED RICE
¼	CUP PLUS 1 TABLESPOON CHOPPED FRESH PARSLEY
1	CUP HEAVY CREAM
¾	CUP LIGHT SOY SAUCE

MELT butter in a large saucepan. Add onions, garlic and dill. Sauté until the onions are translucent, about 5 minutes. Strain tomato juice into the onion mixture. Simmer for 15 minutes.

Meanwhile, puree whole tomatoes, rice and ¼ cup of the parsley in a food processor. With the motor running, add cream and soy sauce in a steady stream. Blend until just combined. Stir into the onion mixture. Simmer for 30 minutes more.

Serve the soup garnished with the remaining 1 tablespoon parsley.

MAKES 4 SERVINGS.

Black Bread

⅓	CUP UNSWEETENED COCOA POWDER
⅓	CUP SUGAR
1	TEASPOON SALT
2	CUPS LUKEWARM COFFEE
2	PACKAGES ACTIVE DRY YEAST
¾	CUP RYE FLOUR
¾	CUP CORN FLOUR
¾	CUP WHOLE WHEAT FLOUR
¾	CUP ALL-PURPOSE FLOUR

COMBINE cocoa powder, sugar and salt. Stir in coffee. Dissolve yeast in the coffee mixture and let stand until the mixture is bubbly, 5 to 8 minutes. Add flours and mix well.

Knead on a lightly floured surface until the dough is smooth and elastic, about 10 minutes. Cover with a damp cloth and let rise in a warm place until doubled in bulk, about 30 minutes.

Preheat oven to 375 degrees F. Lightly oil a baking sheet.

Shape the dough into four rolls and place on the prepared baking sheet. Bake the rolls until the bottoms are browned, about 25 minutes.

MAKES 4 ROLLS.

New England Crab Cakes with Corn & Sweet Pepper Sauce

SAUCE

1	TABLESPOON VEGETABLE OIL
1	MEDIUM TOMATO, PEELED, SEEDED AND CHOPPED
½	CUP FRESH OR FROZEN CORN KERNELS
¼	CUP CHOPPED RED BELL PEPPERS
¼	CUP CHOPPED GREEN BELL PEPPERS
1	TABLESPOON ALL-PURPOSE FLOUR
¼	CUP HEAVY CREAM
1	TABLESPOON CHOPPED FRESH PARSLEY
1	TEASPOON CHOPPED FRESH TARRAGON
2	DASHES OF TABASCO SAUCE
	SALT & FRESHLY GROUND BLACK PEPPER

CRAB CAKES

1¼	POUNDS FRESH MAINE LUMP CRABMEAT, SQUEEZED DRY
½	CUP CRACKER CRUMBS
2	EGGS, LIGHTLY BEATEN
¼	CUP MAYONNAISE
¼	CUP DIJON MUSTARD
2	TABLESPOONS CHOPPED FRESH PARSLEY
1	TABLESPOON VEGETABLE OIL
2	SCALLIONS, FINELY CHOPPED

To PREPARE SAUCE: Heat oil in a saucepan. Add tomatoes, corn and peppers. Sauté until the peppers are soft, about 3 minutes. Add flour and cook, stirring constantly, until golden brown, about 1 minute. Stir in cream, parsley, tarragon and Tabasco. Simmer, stirring, for 5 minutes. Season with salt and pepper to taste. Remove from the heat and cover to keep warm.

TO PREPARE CRAB CAKES: Combine crabmeat, cracker crumbs, eggs, mayonnaise, mustard and parsley. Form into 8 cakes.

Heat oil in a heavy skillet. Sauté the cakes until golden brown, about 2½ minutes each side. Drizzle the sauce over the cakes and garnish with scallions.

MAKES 8 CAKES.

Grilled Venison with Red Wine & Gorgonzola Sauce

½ CUP BEEF STOCK, PREFERABLY HOMEMADE

¼ CUP RED WINE VINEGAR

¼ CUP CATSUP

2 TABLESPOONS DRY RED WINE

2 TABLESPOONS DRY WHITE WINE

1 TEASPOON CRACKED BLACK PEPPERCORNS

1 TEASPOON UNSALTED BUTTER

1 TEASPOON ALL-PURPOSE FLOUR

1 VENISON SADDLE (ABOUT 2 POUNDS)

¼ POUND GORGONZOLA CHEESE, CRUMBLED (1 CUP)

PREPARE a grill.

Combine beef stock, vinegar, catsup, red wine, white wine and peppercorns in a saucepan. Simmer for 20 minutes.

Melt butter in another saucepan. Add flour and cook, stirring constantly, until golden brown. Add to the stock mixture and simmer for 5 minutes.

Meanwhile, grill venison for about 7 minutes each side for medium-rare. Slice the venison thinly and arrange on serving plates. Stir gorgonzola into the stock mixture and spoon the sauce over the venison. (The sauce should be lumpy.) Serve with sautéed zucchini with fresh basil and a puree of beets and fresh dill.

MAKES 4 SERVINGS.

Salmon with Strawberry &
Black Peppercorn Vinaigrette

1	PINT STRAWBERRIES, HULLED
2	TABLESPOONS FINELY CHOPPED ONIONS
¼	CUP VEGETABLE OIL
2	TABLESPOONS FRESHLY GROUND BLACK PEPPER
2	TABLESPOONS WHITE WINE VINEGAR
1	TABLESPOON HONEY
4	6-OUNCE SALMON FILLETS
4	CUPS DRY WHITE WINE
½	LEMON, THINLY SLICED

PREHEAT oven to 450 degrees F.

To make vinaigrette, puree strawberries, onions, oil, pepper, vinegar and honey. Let stand for 15 minutes.

Meanwhile, arrange salmon in a baking dish. Pour wine over the fillets and top with lemon slices. Bake the salmon until it is opaque in the center, 10 to 12 minutes.

Remove the salmon to serving plates. Drizzle the strawberry vinaigrette over the salmon and serve with poached asparagus and a puree of carrots and fresh cilantro.

MAKES 4 SERVINGS.

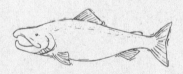

Raspberry Gratin

¼	CUP SUGAR
1	EGG YOLK, WELL BEATEN
2	TABLESPOONS ALL-PURPOSE FLOUR
½	CUP MILK
½	CUP HEAVY CREAM
½	TEASPOON PURE VANILLA EXTRACT
¼	CUP MASCARPONE CHEESE
1	PINT RASPBERRIES
	CONFECTIONERS' SUGAR FOR DUSTING

PREHEAT oven to 500 degrees F.

Gradually beat sugar into egg yolk. Fold in flour.

Heat milk almost to a boil. Pour over the egg mixture and mix well. Return to the pan and boil, stirring constantly, for 2 minutes.

Pour the custard into a bowl and set over a larger bowl filled with ice cubes. Stir vigorously to thicken the custard.

Whip cream and vanilla until stiff peaks begin to form. Fold the whipped cream and mascarpone cheese into the custard until just combined.

Arrange the berries in the bottom of a soufflé dish. Pour the custard over the berries. Bake the gratin until golden brown, 6 to 8 minutes.

Serve the gratin dusted with confectioners' sugar.

MAKES 4 SERVINGS.

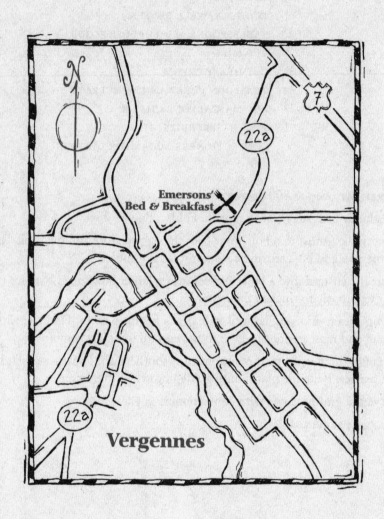

**Emersons'
Bed & Breakfast** ✕

22a

7

N

22a

Vergennes

Emersons'
Bed & Breakfast

82 Main Street
Vergennes, Vermont 05491
(802) 877-3293

TWO ACRES OF LAWNS, gardens and fruit trees surround this home that dates from the 1850s. Inside, guests relax in the Victorian parlor or in one of the six comfortable guest rooms named after New England authors. The home has been restored to preserve its original features—three fireplaces, pocket doors, pine flooring and stained and leaded glass windows. In summer, enjoy lemonade on the veranda and enjoy views of the Adirondack and Green Mountains, or sip hot chocolate in front of the fire in winter.

NEARBY & NOTEWORTHY: Kennedy Brothers Factory Marketplace, just a short walk from the bed and breakfast, houses a number of independent shops that sell everything from antiques to Vermont products. Originally, the building was owned by two brothers—the Kennedys—who manufactured wooden bowls, trays and other wood products. These products are still manufactured today.

New Orleans Beignets

Raspberry Crumble Muffins

Mushroom Quiche

Easy Napoleons

New Orleans Beignets

½   CUP ALL-PURPOSE FLOUR
½   TEASPOON SUGAR
¼   TEASPOON SALT
4   TABLESPOONS LIGHTLY SALTED BUTTER,
     CUT INTO BITS
2   EGGS, LIGHTLY BEATEN
     VEGETABLE OIL FOR DEEP-FRYING
     CONFECTIONERS' SUGAR FOR DUSTING

SIFT flour, sugar and salt into a bowl.

Heat butter and 1 cup water over low heat until the butter is melted. Bring to a boil. Remove from the heat. Add the flour mixture and stir vigorously until a smooth paste forms. Set the pan over medium heat and stir until the dough begins to pull away from the sides of the pan, about 5 minutes. Remove from the heat and let cool for 5 minutes.

Beat one-quarter of the eggs at a time into the dough. Beat until the dough is smooth and shiny.

Pour 2 to 3 inches of oil into a large, deep heavy skillet or deep-fryer. Heat until the oil registers 375 degrees F on a deep-frying thermometer. Dip a tablespoon in the hot oil and use to scoop the dough into the skillet. Fry in batches until puffed and golden brown, about 6 minutes. Drain on paper towels.

Serve the beignets hot dusted with confectioners' sugar.

MAKES ABOUT 12 BEIGNETS.

Raspberry Crumble Muffins

These muffins are best when prepared with just-picked raspberries.

TOPPING

¼	CUP FINELY CHOPPED PECANS
¼	CUP PACKED DARK BROWN SUGAR
3	TABLESPOONS ALL-PURPOSE FLOUR
1	TEASPOON GROUND CINNAMON
3	TABLESPOONS LIGHTLY SALTED BUTTER, MELTED

MUFFINS

1½	CUPS ALL-PURPOSE FLOUR
¼	CUP SUGAR
¼	CUP PACKED LIGHT BROWN SUGAR
2	TEASPOONS BAKING POWDER
1	TEASPOON GROUND CINNAMON
⅛	TEASPOON SALT
1	EGG, LIGHTLY BEATEN
¼	POUND (1 STICK) LIGHTLY SALTED BUTTER, MELTED
½	CUP MILK
1¼	CUPS FRESH RASPBERRIES
	GRATED ZEST OF 1 LEMON

TO PREPARE TOPPING: Combine pecans, brown sugar, flour and cinnamon. Stir in melted butter.

TO PREPARE MUFFINS: Preheat oven to 350 degrees F. Grease a 12-cup muffin tin.

Sift flour into a bowl. Stir in sugar, brown sugar, baking powder, cinnamon and salt. Make a well in the flour mixture and add egg, melted butter and milk. Stir until just combined. Fold in raspberries and lemon zest.

Divide the batter evenly among the prepared muffin cups. Sprinkle the topping over each muffin. Bake the muffins until golden brown and a tester comes out clean, about 25 minutes.

MAKES 12 MUFFINS.

Mushroom Quiche

CRUST

¼	POUND (1 STICK) LIGHTLY SALTED BUTTER
1	CUP FLOUR

FILLING

2	TABLESPOONS OLIVE OIL
1	TABLESPOON LIGHTLY SALTED BUTTER
1	POUND MUSHROOMS, TRIMMED AND THINLY SLICED
1	CLOVE GARLIC, FINELY CHOPPED
	JUICE OF ½ LEMON
	SALT & GROUND BLACK PEPPER
2	TABLESPOONS FINELY CHOPPED FRESH PARSLEY OR 2 TEASPOONS DRIED PARSLEY FLAKES
3	EGGS
1½	CUPS WHIPPING CREAM
⅛	POUND PARMESAN CHEESE, GRATED (½ CUP)

TO PREPARE CRUST: Cream butter and flour. Mix in 2 to 3 tablespoons of cold water so that the mixture holds together and is not dry. Form into a ball, wrap in wax paper and refrigerate for at least 3 hours.

Preheat oven to 375 degrees F.

Press the dough into a 10-inch pie or tart pan. Bake the crust until golden brown, about 15 minutes. Prepare the filling while the crust is baking.

TO PREPARE FILLING: Heat oil and butter in a skillet until the butter is melted. Stir in mushrooms, garlic and lemon juice. Season with salt and pepper to taste. Sauté until the mushrooms release their liquid. Raise the heat and sauté until the liquid is evaporated. Stir in parsley. Remove from the heat.

Whisk together eggs and cream in a large bowl. Add the mushroom mixture and stir.

Sprinkle the crust with Parmesan. Pour the mushroom filling into the crust. Bake the quiche until golden brown, about 30 minutes.

MAKES ONE 10-INCH QUICHE.

Easy Napoleons

¾ CUP WHIPPING CREAM

3 TABLESPOONS INSTANT COCOA

1 TEASPOON MILK (MORE OR LESS TO REACH
   DESIRED CONSISTENCY)

1 BOX (1 POUND) GRAHAM CRACKERS

1 PACKAGE (3.4 OUNCES) INSTANT VANILLA PUDDING,
   PREPARED USING ONLY 1½ CUPS MILK

3 TABLESPOONS CONFECTIONERS' SUGAR

WHIP cream until soft peaks begin to form. In another bowl, blend cocoa with milk.

Arrange one layer of graham crackers in a 9 x 13-inch glass dish. Spread prepared pudding over the graham crackers. Arrange another layer of graham crackers over the pudding. Top with the whipped cream and another layer of graham crackers.

Stir together confectioners' sugar and 1 teaspoon water. Spread over the graham crackers. Decoratively drizzle the cocoa mixture over the sugar topping. Refrigerate for at least 3 hours before serving.

MAKES ONE 9 X 13-INCH CAKE.

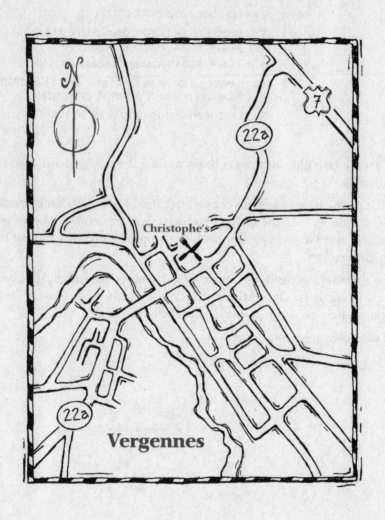

Christophe's

Vergennes

Christophe's

5 Green Street
Vergennes, Vermont 05491
(802) 877-3413

SITUATED in the historic Stevens House overlooking the Green, this chef-owned restaurant serves innovative French country fare. Dishes are prepared using the freshest of local products and are served in an intimate yet relaxed setting from May through October.

NEARBY & NOTEWORTHY: Rokeby Museum in Ferrisburgh is just a short drive north on Route 7. Originally a stop on the underground railroad for slaves escaping to Canada, Rokeby was home to four generations of Robinsons from the 1790s to the 1960s. Rowland Evans Robinson, who lived at Rokeby until the turn of the century, was a skillful writer and artist. He is well known for his use of the Vermont dialect in the Danvis Tales, his stories of early Vermont. The family's belongings, including some of their literary and artistic works, are on display at the homestead.

Artichoke & Celery Soup

Salad Gracianne

Escalope à la Foyot

Crêpes Mousseline

Artichoke & Celery Soup

6   CELERY STALKS, SLICED (3 CUPS)
4   ARTICHOKE HEARTS, PREFERABLY FRESH
2   CUPS CHICKEN STOCK, PREFERABLY HOMEMADE
⅓   CUP DRY WHITE WINE
1½   TEASPOONS DRY MUSTARD
1   CUP HALF-AND-HALF OR LIGHT CREAM
⅛   TEASPOON FRESHLY GRATED NUTMEG
     SALT & GROUND BLACK PEPPER
     CELERY SEEDS FOR GARNISH

PLACE celery, artichoke hearts, chicken stock, 1 cup water, wine and mustard in a large saucepan. Cover and simmer until the vegetables are very soft, about 30 minutes.

Puree the soup in a food processor or blender, in batches if necessary. Stir in half-and-half or light cream and nutmeg. Season with salt and pepper to taste.

Garnish the soup with celery seeds and serve with poppy seed crackers.

MAKES 4 SERVINGS.

Salad Gracianne

SALAD

4	MEDIUM VERY RIPE TOMATOES
½	TEASPOON SEA SALT
1	HEAD BIBB LETTUCE, SEPARATED INTO LEAVES, WASHED AND DRIED
1	HEAD ROMAINE LETTUCE, SEPARATED INTO LEAVES, WASHED AND DRIED
4	BASIL LEAVES OR ½ CUP ITALIAN PARSLEY

DRESSING

1½	TEASPOONS DIJON MUSTARD
1½	TEASPOONS RICE VINEGAR
1½	TEASPOONS RED WINE VINEGAR
⅛	TEASPOON SALT
½	CUP SAFFLOWER OIL
¼	CUP PINE NUTS

TO PREPARE SALAD: Cut each tomato into 5 slices. Finely chop the 8 end slices. Sprinkle the remaining slices with salt. Let drain in a colander for 2 hours.

Cut off and discard the white part at the base of the large lettuce leaves. Fold leaves in half and cut into strips. Fold basil leaves in half, if using, and cut into strips. Toss the lettuce and the basil or parsley with the chopped tomatoes.

TO PREPARE DRESSING: Whisk together mustard, vinegars and salt. Add oil and 2 tablespoons water in a steady stream, whisking constantly until well combined.

TO ASSEMBLE SALAD: Arrange 3 tomato slices on each plate in a cloverleaf pattern. Lightly brush the tomato slices with the dressing. Toss the lettuce mixture with the remaining dressing. Mound on top of the sliced tomatoes. Garnish the salad with pine nuts.

MAKES 4 SERVINGS.

Escalope à la Foyot

¾   POUND SHALLOTS, PEELED
2   TABLESPOONS LIGHTLY SALTED BUTTER
4   ½-INCH-THICK VEAL SCALOPPINE
½   CUP FRESH UNSEASONED BREADCRUMBS
⅛   POUND SWISS CHEESE, GRATED (½ CUP)
1   CUP DRY WHITE WINE

PREHEAT oven to 400 degrees F. Lightly oil a baking dish.

Boil shallots in salted water to cover for 1 minute. Plunge into cold water. Return shallots to boiling water and cook for 1 minute more. Plunge into cold water again. When cool enough to handle, finely chop the shallots.

Melt 1 tablespoon of the butter in a skillet over high heat. When the skillet is very hot, sear scaloppine until white on both sides. Remove to a plate. Reduce heat to low and add the remaining 1 tablespoon butter and the shallots. Cook, stirring, over low heat until the shallots are very soft, about 5 minutes.

Spread 1 tablespoon of the shallot mixture over each scaloppine. Mix together breadcrumbs and cheese. Spread evenly over the shallot mixture.

Place scaloppine in the prepared baking dish. Bake until the edges of the scaloppine begin to brown, about 5 minutes. Pour wine into the dish and bake until the cheese is lightly browned, 5 to 10 minutes more. Cover with aluminum foil and bake the scaloppine for 20 minutes more.

MAKES 4 SERVINGS.

Crêpes Mousseline

3	EGGS, SEPARATED
5½	TABLESPOONS UNSALTED BUTTER, MELTED
¾	CUP FLOUR
2	CUPS MILK
½	CUP SUGAR
4	TABLESPOONS UNSALTED BUTTER

BEAT egg yolks and melted butter until well combined. Add flour and mix well. Add milk in a steady stream and whisk until smooth. Whisk in sugar. Set aside for 1 hour.

Beat egg whites until stiff. Spread on the surface of the batter.

Heat a nonstick skillet over medium heat. Add ½ tablespoon of the butter and let melt. Ladle one-eighth of the batter into the skillet (be sure to include some of the egg white). Sauté the crêpe on one side until golden brown, about 1 minute. Roll the crêpe with a spatula and place seam-side down on a serving plate. Repeat with the remaining batter, melting more butter before cooking each crêpe.

MAKES 8 CRÊPES.

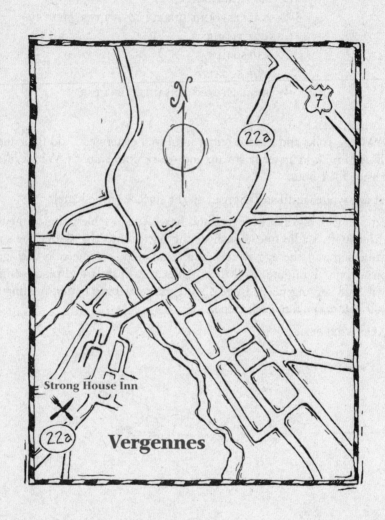

Strong House Inn

Vergennes

Strong House Inn

82 West Main Street
Vergennes, Vermont 05491
(802) 877-3337

STRONG HOUSE INN, an 1834 Federal home listed on the National Register of Historic Places, is located on a hillcrest with panoramic views of the Adirondack and Green Mountains. The area has some of the finest cycling routes in Vermont, and walking trails lead from the inn into the surrounding countryside. A full country breakfast is served only to overnight guests, but those who call for reservations can enjoy Sunday afternoon tea.

NEARBY & NOTEWORTHY: MacDonough Wharf, at the base of Otter Creek Falls in Vergennes, is named after Captain Thomas MacDonough, who assembled the United States fleet near here during the War of 1812. Although outnumbered and outgunned by the British, his fleet soundly defeated them on Lake Champlain near Plattsburgh, New York.

Walnut & Currant Scones

Madeleines

Walnut & Currant Scones

Serve these scones warm or at room temperature with butter and jam.

3	CUPS ALL-PURPOSE FLOUR
¼	CUP SUGAR
1	TABLESPOON BAKING POWDER
½	TEASPOON SALT
5	TABLESPOONS UNSALTED BUTTER, CUT INTO BITS
2	EGGS
1¼	CUPS MILK
¾	CUP CHOPPED WALNUTS
¼	CUP DRIED CURRANTS
1	EGG YOLK

PREHEAT oven to 350 degrees F. Butter 2 baking sheets.

Sift flour, sugar, baking powder and salt into a large bowl. Distribute butter over the flour mixture and blend until the mixture resembles coarse meal. Beat eggs and milk until well combined. Add to the flour mixture and mix well. Fold in walnuts and currants.

Use an ice cream scoop to spoon the dough onto the prepared baking sheets. Beat egg yolk with 2 tablespoons water. Brush each scone with the egg yolk mixture and bake until golden brown, about 20 minutes.

MAKES 12 SCONES.

Madeleines

2	EGGS, AT ROOM TEMPERATURE
¾	TEASPOON SALT
⅓	CUP SUGAR
½	TEASPOON PURE VANILLA EXTRACT
½	CUP ALL-PURPOSE FLOUR
4	TABLESPOONS UNSALTED BUTTER, MELTED

ARRANGE an oven rack in the lowest position and preheat oven to 400 degrees F. Butter and flour two 12-mold madeleine pans.

In a large bowl, beat eggs and salt. Gradually add sugar and beat until stiff peaks form. Stir in vanilla. Sift flour into the egg mixture in four parts, folding in after each addition. Add 1 tablespoon of the melted butter at a time, folding in immediately after each addition.

Divide the batter evenly among the prepared madeleine molds. Bake the madeleines until the edges are browned and the tops are golden, 10 to 15 minutes.

MAKES 24 MADELEINES.

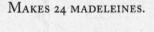

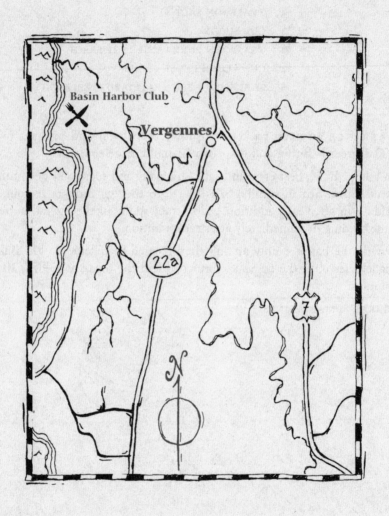

Basin Harbor Club

Vergennes

22a

7

N

Basin Harbor Club

Basin Harbor Road
Vergennes, Vermont 05491
(802) 475-2311/(800) 622-4000

THIS SEASONAL RESORT has been owned and operated by the Beach family since 1886. The approach to the club is through cornfields and pastures of black and white cows. As you pass through the club's entrance, however, you enter a different world. The resort is set on the shores of Lake Champlain. Guests stay in small cottages scattered throughout the grounds—some are facing the golf course or adjacent to the pool, others are along the walking paths or perched on the edge of the bluff overlooking Lake Champlain. The following menu is representative of the cuisine served in the main dining room, one of the resort's three restaurants.

NEARBY & NOTEWORTHY: Within easy walking distance of Basin Harbor is the Lake Champlain Maritime Museum. Learn about the lake's history through the museum's historical exhibits and maritime collection.

Polenta Timbale with Vermont Goat Cheese

Chilled Strawberry & Rhubarb Soup

Baby Field Greens with Olive Paste Crostini

Herb–Dijon–Crusted Rack of Lamb

Garlic Mashed Yukon Gold Potatoes

Ragoût of Ramps & Fiddlehead Ferns

Crème Brûlée

Polenta Timbale with Vermont Goat Cheese

VINAIGRETTE

	JUICE OF 2 LEMONS
1	SHALLOT, THINLY SLICED
⅓	CUP VEGETABLE OIL
⅓	CUP OLIVE OIL
	PINCH OF SALT
2	TABLESPOONS CHOPPED FRESH THYME

POLENTA & SALAD

2¼	CUPS HALF-AND-HALF
1	CUP CORNMEAL
¼	POUND VERMONT GOAT CHEESE, CRUMBLED (1 CUP)
2	TABLESPOONS CHOPPED FRESH HERBS (DILL, PARSLEY, CHERVIL, ROSEMARY)
1	CUP DRY UNSEASONED BREADCRUMBS
1½	CUPS OLIVE OIL
4	HEADS BABY FRISÉE, WASHED, DRIED AND CUT IN HALF (LEAVE ROOT INTACT)

TO PREPARE VINAIGRETTE: Heat lemon juice in a small saucepan over high heat for 1 minute. Remove from the heat. Stir in shallots, vegetable oil, olive oil and salt. Let cool to room temperature. Stir in thyme.

TO PREPARE POLENTA: Lightly oil 8 small ramekins.

In a large heavy saucepan, gradually stir half-and-half into cornmeal. Simmer, stirring constantly, for 3 minutes. Remove from the heat and fold in goat cheese and herbs. Pour into the prepared ramekins and let chill for about 1 hour.

Preheat oven to 400 degrees F. Unmold polenta and dredge with breadcrumbs.

Heat oil in a skillet over medium-high heat. Fry the polenta until lightly browned. Remove from the skillet and drain on paper towels. Arrange on a baking sheet and bake the polenta for 10 minutes.

TO ASSEMBLE SALAD: Arrange a frisée half on each plate, top with a polenta mold and sprinkle with the vinaigrette.

MAKES 8 SERVINGS.

Chilled Strawberry & Rhubarb Soup

3   PINTS STRAWBERRIES, HULLED AND SLICED
2   CUPS PEELED AND CHOPPED FRESH RHUBARB
½   CUP SUGAR
2   CUPS ORANGE JUICE
2   CUPS PLAIN YOGURT
    HONEY
    FRESH MINT SPRIGS FOR GARNISH

COMBINE strawberries, rhubarb and sugar in a bowl. Let marinate for 8 hours.

In a blender or food processor, puree the strawberry mixture and orange juice. Whisk in yogurt and honey to taste.

Ladle the soup into chilled bowls and garnish with mint.

MAKES 8 SERVINGS.

Baby Field Greens with Olive Paste Crostini

8   ¼-INCH-THICK ROUNDS FRENCH BREAD
     OLIVE OIL FOR BRUSHING BREAD
1   CUP KALAMATA OLIVES, PITTED
8   CUPS WASHED AND DRIED MESCLUN (ARUGULA,
         CHERVIL, GREEN OAK LEAF LETTUCE, LOLLO
         ROSSA, MÂCHE, MIZUNA, RED OAK LEAF
         LETTUCE, TAT-SOI)
½   CUP OLIVE OIL
¼   CUP BALSAMIC VINEGAR

To MAKE crostini, brush both sides of bread with oil. Toast or grill the bread until golden brown.

Puree olives in a blender or food processor. Spread one side of the crostini with the olive puree.

Arrange mesclun on 8 plates, sprinkle with oil and vinegar and top with the crostini.

MAKES 8 SERVINGS.

Herb–Dijon–Crusted Rack of Lamb

4	8-BONE LAMB RACKS, FRENCHED AND CUT IN HALF
½	CUP DIJON MUSTARD
1	CUP DRY UNSEASONED BREADCRUMBS
2	TABLESPOONS CHOPPED FRESH PARSLEY
2	CUPS LAMB OR CHICKEN STOCK, PREFERABLY HOMEMADE
	FRESH ROSEMARY SPRIG
	SALT & GROUND BLACK PEPPER

PREHEAT oven to 400 degrees F.

In a large skillet, sear lamb racks on all sides until browned. Remove from the heat and brush with mustard.

Combine breadcrumbs and parsley. Coat the lamb racks with the breadcrumb mixture. Transfer the lamb to a roasting pan and cover the bone ends with aluminum foil. Roast the lamb for about 20 minutes for medium-rare. Remove to a plate and loosely cover with aluminum foil to keep warm.

Pour lamb or chicken stock into the roasting pan. To reduce the sauce, cook over high heat, gently scraping the brown bits from the bottom and sides of the pan, for 3 to 4 minutes. Add rosemary and simmer until reduced by two-thirds. Strain the sauce through a fine sieve into a bowl. Season with salt and pepper to taste.

Arrange the lamb on serving plates and spoon the sauce on top.

MAKES 8 SERVINGS.

Garlic Mashed
Yukon Gold Potatoes

8   LARGE YUKON GOLD POTATOES (ABOUT 2 POUNDS),
       PEELED AND CUBED
8   CLOVES GARLIC, FINELY CHOPPED
1   CUP OLIVE OIL
      SALT & GROUND BLACK PEPPER

Boil potatoes in salted water to cover until tender, about 10 minutes. Drain and mash.

Sauté garlic in oil until fragrant but not browned. Add the oil mixture to the potatoes and mix well. Season with salt and pepper to taste.

MAKES 8 SERVINGS.

Ragoût of Ramps
& Fiddlehead Ferns

1   POUND FIDDLEHEAD FERNS
2   TABLESPOONS OLIVE OIL
1   POUND RAMPS, OR WILD LEEKS,
       CUT INTO JULIENNE
      SALT & GROUND BLACK PEPPER

Boil fiddleheads in salted water to cover until tender, about 2 minutes. Plunge into cold water to stop cooking. Drain well.

Heat oil in a skillet over medium-high heat. Add ramps and the fiddleheads and sauté until tender, 3 to 5 minutes. Season with salt and pepper to taste.

MAKES 8 SERVINGS.

Crème Brûlée

8	EGG YOLKS
½	CUP SUGAR
2	CUPS HEAVY CREAM
2	CUPS MILK
1	SMALL VANILLA BEAN, CUT IN HALF LENGTHWISE
½	CUP UNPACKED LIGHT BROWN SUGAR, SIFTED

WHISK egg yolks and sugar until ribbons begin to form, about 5 minutes.

In a saucepan, bring cream, milk and vanilla bean to a boil. Remove from the heat. Scrape the vanilla bean seeds into the mixture and discard the bean.

Whisk one-half of the cream mixture into the egg mixture. Then whisk the cream-egg mixture into the remaining cream mixture. Cook over low heat, stirring constantly with a wooden spoon, until thickened, 15 to 20 minutes. (Do not simmer as the mixture will separate.) Ladle the custard into 8 ramekins and chill until set, about 2 hours.

Just before serving, preheat broiler. Sprinkle each ramekin with 1 tablespoon of the brown sugar. Broil the custard until the sugar is lightly browned, about 2 minutes.

MAKES 8 SERVINGS.

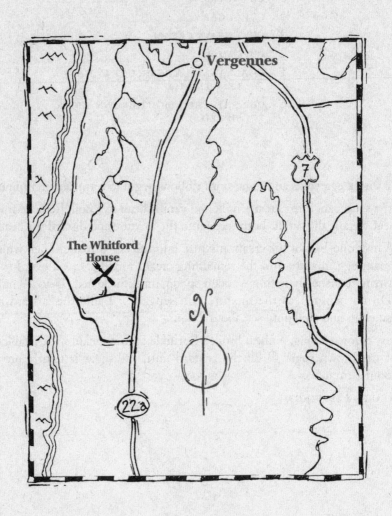

Vergennes

7

The Whitford
House

N

22a

The Whitford House

Grandey Road
RR 1, Box 1490
Vergennes, Vermont 05491
(802) 758-2704/(800) 746-2704

THIS 1790S INN is located on a country lane just a few miles from Lake Champlain. From the shaded veranda and sunny deck, guests enjoy vistas of rolling hills and the distant Adirondack Mountains. Inside, there are wood-burning fireplaces, a well-stocked library and comfortable guest rooms with views of the surrounding countryside.

NEARBY & NOTEWORTHY: Visit Chimney Point, the site of early Native American campsites and French Colonial settlements. Then cross the Lake Champlain Bridge to Crown Point, the site of a Revolutionary War fortress. While just the remains of the fort are visible, there is an informative slide show at the Visitor's Center that explores the military history of Lake Champlain.

Honey–Coconut Granola

Stewed Apples

Crab Cakes

California Frittata

Belgian Waffles

Honey–Coconut Granola

2	CUPS ORGANIC OLD-FASHIONED ROLLED OATS
⅔	CUP UNSWEETENED SHREDDED COCONUT
⅓	CUP RAW SUNFLOWER SEEDS
⅓	CUP UNHULLED SESAME SEEDS
⅓	CUP RAW WHEAT GERM
⅓	CUP CHOPPED RAW ALMONDS
⅓	CUP RAISINS
1	TEASPOON GROUND CINNAMON
½	CUP LIQUID (UNCRYSTALLIZED) HONEY
¼	CUP CANOLA OIL

PREHEAT oven to 300 degrees F.

Combine oats, coconut, sunflower seeds, sesame seeds, wheat germ, almonds, raisins and cinnamon. Add honey and oil and mix well.

Spread the mixture evenly on 2 baking sheets. Bake the granola, stirring frequently, until golden brown, 45 to 60 minutes. Stir occasionally while cooling. Serve with milk or yogurt.

MAKES 6 SERVINGS.

Stewed Apples

This versatile dish may be served on its own or as a topping for waffles, pancakes or granola.

10	MACINTOSH APPLES, PEELED, CORED AND CUT INTO QUARTERS
3	TABLESPOONS PACKED LIGHT BROWN SUGAR
1	TABLESPOON CHOPPED CRYSTALLIZED GINGER
1½	TEASPOONS GROUND CINNAMON

IN A LARGE saucepan, simmer apples, ½ cup water, brown sugar, ginger and cinnamon until the apples are tender, about 15 minutes.

MAKES 6 SERVINGS.

Crab Cakes

¼   POUND (1 STICK) UNSALTED BUTTER
¼   CUP FINELY CHOPPED ONIONS
⅓   CUP FINELY CHOPPED CELERY
3   EGGS
¾   CUP FRESH SEASONED BREADCRUMBS
¾   CUP HEAVY CREAM
3   TABLESPOONS CHOPPED ITALIAN PARSLEY
    JUICE OF 1 SMALL LEMON
1   TABLESPOON DIJON MUSTARD
1½   POUNDS FRESH FLAKED CRABMEAT, SQUEEZED DRY
    SALT & GROUND BLACK PEPPER
3   LEMONS OR LIMES, CUT INTO WEDGES
    CHOPPED FRESH CILANTRO FOR GARNISH

MELT 3 tablespoons of the butter in a skillet. Add onions and sauté until translucent, about 3 minutes. Add celery and sauté for 3 minutes more. Remove from the heat and let cool.

Beat eggs in a large bowl. Add breadcrumbs, cream, the onion mixture, parsley, lemon juice and mustard. Mix well. Stir in crabmeat and season with salt and pepper to taste. Chill for at least 3 hours.

Form into 6 cakes. Dust lightly with flour.

Melt the remaining 5 tablespoons butter in a heavy skillet. Sauté the cakes until golden brown, 4 to 5 minutes each side.

Serve the crab cakes with lemon or lime wedges and garnish with cilantro.

MAKES 6 CAKES.

California Frittata

*Transform this dish into a south-of-the-border specialty by serving it
with salsa, sour cream and guacamole.*

1	POUND HOT OR MILD SAUSAGES, CASINGS REMOVED, CRUMBLED
3	TABLESPOONS OLIVE OIL
½	POUND MUSHROOMS, TRIMMED AND SLICED
1	MEDIUM ONION, CHOPPED
1¼	CUPS CHOPPED, SLICED OR JULIENNED VEGETABLES (EGGPLANT, ZUCCHINI, BELL PEPPERS, BROCCOLI, YELLOW SQUASH)
6	EGGS, LIGHTLY BEATEN
¼	POUND PARMESAN CHEESE, GRATED (1 CUP)
2	CLOVES GARLIC, FINELY CHOPPED
½	TEASPOON CHOPPED FRESH BASIL
¼	TEASPOON CHOPPED FRESH MARJORAM
	SALT & GROUND BLACK PEPPER
1	LARGE TOMATO, THINLY SLICED
¼	POUND MOZZARELLA CHEESE, GRATED (1 CUP)

PREHEAT oven to 350 degrees F. Butter a 9-inch pie pan.

Brown sausage in a skillet. Remove to drain on paper towels. Wipe out the skillet and add oil; heat oil over medium-high heat. Add mushrooms and onions and sauté until softened, about 3 minutes. Add other vegetables and sauté until softened, about 5 minutes.

Combine eggs, ¾ cup of the Parmesan, garlic, basil and marjoram. Season with salt and pepper to taste. Stir in the sausage and the sautéed vegetables.

Pour the egg mixture into the prepared pie pan and arrange tomatoes on top. Combine the remaining ¼ cup Parmesan and mozzarella and sprinkle over the top. Bake the frittata until set, 20 to 25 minutes.

MAKES 6 SERVINGS.

Belgian Waffles

3   EGGS, SEPARATED
¾   CUP MILK
¾   CUP LIGHT SOUR CREAM
¼   POUND (1 STICK) UNSALTED BUTTER, MELTED
1   TEASPOON PURE VANILLA EXTRACT
1½   CUPS SIFTED ALL-PURPOSE FLOUR
2   TEASPOONS BAKING POWDER
½   TEASPOON BAKING SODA
½   TEASPOON SALT
1   EGG WHITE

LIGHTLY oil and preheat a waffle iron.

In a large bowl, beat egg yolks until frothy. Beat in milk, sour cream, melted butter and vanilla. Sift together flour, baking powder, baking soda and salt. Gradually beat into the sour cream mixture until well combined.

In another bowl, beat the 4 egg whites until stiff. Gently fold into the batter.

Cook the waffles in the prepared waffle iron until golden brown, about 2 minutes. Drizzle maple syrup over the waffles and serve with fresh pork sausage or maple-smoked bacon.

MAKES 6 SERVINGS.

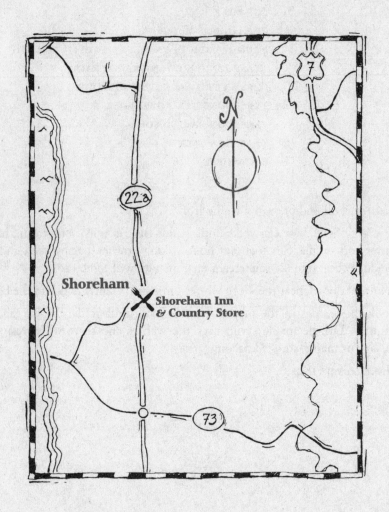

Shoreham

Shoreham Inn & Country Store

Shoreham Inn & Country Store

Route 74
Shoreham, Vermont 05770
(802) 897-5081/(800) 255-5081

SHOREHAM INN & COUNTRY STORE is a 200-year-old lodging establishment overlooking the Green in this quaint, historic village. There are 11 guest rooms and common areas filled with country antiques. Guests dine in a room with exposed beams in front of the fireplace. A visit to the adjacent country store will lead you back in time. Before the age of the automobile, people depended on country stores to supply everything from toothpaste, milk and bread to stovepipes, kerosene lamps and clothing. Shoreham Country Store still exhibits this range of merchandise, and it is now also known for its fine deli.

NEARBY & NOTEWORTHY: Just north of the junction of Route 22A and Route 74 is the old stone one-room schoolhouse. Built in 1839, it is now occupied by the Shoreham Historical Society. Visitors can learn about the area's history through the displays of local artifacts.

Russian Cabbage Soup

Roasted Chicken with Pineapple

Fruited Baby Carrots

Double Fudge Bars with Walnut Icing

Russian Cabbage Soup

2	CANS (28 OUNCES EACH) STEWED TOMATOES
1	HEAD GREEN CABBAGE, CORED AND CHOPPED
1	SMALL ONION, CHOPPED
¾	CUP RAISINS
½	CUP PACKED DARK BROWN SUGAR
1	BAY LEAF
	DRIED MINCED GARLIC
	GROUND BLACK PEPPER

PUREE tomatoes in a blender or food processor, in batches if necessary.

Combine the pureed tomatoes, 4 cups water, cabbage and onions in a large pot. Simmer for 30 minutes.

Stir in raisins, brown sugar and bay leaf. Season with dried garlic and pepper to taste. Simmer until the cabbage is tender, about 1 hour more.

Discard bay leaf before serving.

MAKES 8 SERVINGS.

Roasted Chicken with Pineapple

1	LARGE ONION
2	2½-POUND FRYER CHICKENS, CUT INTO QUARTERS
1	CAN (20 OUNCES) CRUSHED PINEAPPLE, WITH JUICE
¼	CUP ORANGE MARMALADE
2	TABLESPOONS RED WINE VINEGAR
	DRIED MINCED GARLIC
	GROUND BLACK PEPPER

THINLY slice one-half of the onion; finely chop the remaining one-half. Layer the thinly sliced onions in a roasting pan. Top with chicken. Stir together the chopped onions, pineapple, marmalade and vinegar. Season with dried garlic and pepper to taste. Pour over the chicken, cover and let marinate in the refrigerator for 3 hours.

Preheat oven to 350 degrees F.

Bake the chicken, turning every 30 minutes, until it is very tender and no longer pink inside, about 2 hours. Serve over egg noodles.

MAKES 8 SERVINGS.

Fruited Baby Carrots

2	POUNDS BABY CARROTS
4	LARGE APPLES, CORED AND CUT INTO 1-INCH CUBES
2	CUPS RAISINS
4	CUPS ORANGE JUICE
¾	CUP PURE VERMONT MAPLE SYRUP

BOIL carrots in salted water to cover until tender, about 15 minutes.

Drain the carrots. Return to the pot and add apples, raisins, orange juice and maple syrup. Simmer over low heat until the carrots are very tender, 30 to 45 minutes.

MAKES 8 SERVINGS.

Double Fudge Bars with Walnut Icing

FUDGE BARS

2   CUPS ALL-PURPOSE FLOUR
2   CUPS SUGAR
1   CUP CANOLA OIL
¼   CUP UNSWEETENED COCOA POWDER
2   EGGS, WELL BEATEN
½   CUP SOUR CREAM
1   TEASPOON BAKING SODA

WALNUT ICING

2½   CUPS CONFECTIONERS' SUGAR
1   CUP CHOPPED WALNUTS
1   TEASPOON PURE VANILLA EXTRACT
½   CUP CANOLA OIL
⅓   CUP HALF-AND-HALF
¼   CUP UNSWEETENED COCOA POWDER

TO PREPARE FUDGE BARS: Preheat oven to 375 degrees F. Lightly butter a 9 x 13-inch baking dish.

Combine flour and sugar in a large bowl. Heat oil, 1 cup water and cocoa powder over medium-high heat, stirring constantly until well blended. Add to the flour mixture and mix well. Stir in eggs, sour cream and baking soda. (The mixture will be runny.)

Pour the batter into the prepared pan. Bake the bars until they spring back when lightly touched, about 30 minutes. While the bars are baking, make the icing.

TO PREPARE WALNUT ICING: Combine confectioners' sugar, walnuts and vanilla. Heat oil, half-and-half and cocoa powder almost to a boil, stirring constantly. Add to the sugar mixture and stir until smooth. Immediately spread on the warm bars. Cut into 4 x 2-inch sections.

Serve the bars warm topped with ice cream, fudge sauce and whipped cream.

MAKES ABOUT 16 BARS.

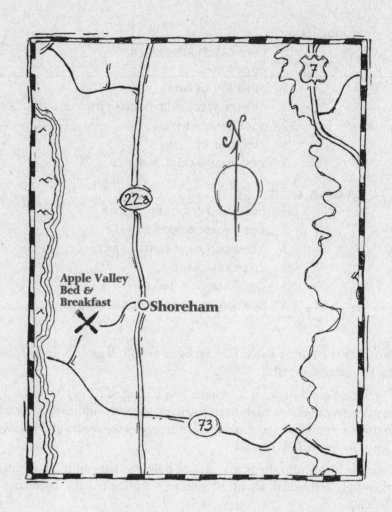

Apple Valley Bed & Breakfast

Shoreham

Apple Valley
Bed & Breakfast

Box 45, Smith Street
Shoreham, Vermont 05770
(802) 897-7621

LOCATED JUST OUTSIDE the historic town of Shoreham, Apple Valley is a small bed and breakfast overlooking Lake Champlain and the Adirondack Mountains. The original home was built in the late 1700s; attached is the Federal main house, which is listed on the Vermont State Register of Historic Places. There are roughly a dozen orchards in the neighborhood that produce as many as 500,000 bushels of apples each year. When in season, apples from neighboring orchards are used in some of the recipes prepared for guests.

NEARBY & NOTEWORTHY: A short trip southwest from the property will lead you to Larrabee's Point, a Lake Champlain ferry crossing since the 1700s. Here, you can hop on a ferry that will carry you to the New York side of the lake. Fort Ticonderoga, a restored Revolutionary War fortress, is just at the crest of the hill.

Oatmeal Apple Raisin Muffins

Cheddar Soufflé

Oatmeal Apple Raisin Muffins

1	EGG, LIGHTLY BEATEN
¾	CUP MILK
½	CUP VEGETABLE OIL
1	CUP ALL-PURPOSE FLOUR
⅓	CUP SUGAR
1	TABLESPOON BAKING POWDER
1	TEASPOON GROUND CINNAMON
1	TEASPOON SALT
½	TEASPOON GROUND NUTMEG
1	CUP QUICK-COOKING ROLLED OATS
1	CUP RAISINS
1	APPLE (SUCH AS MACINTOSH), PEELED, CORED AND CHOPPED

PREHEAT oven to 400 degrees F. Lightly oil a 12-cup muffin tin.

Beat egg, milk and oil in a large bowl until well combined. Sift together flour, sugar, baking powder, cinnamon, salt and nutmeg. Fold into the egg mixture until just combined. Stir in oats, raisins and apples.

Divide the batter evenly among the prepared muffin cups. Bake the muffins until golden brown and a tester comes out clean, 15 to 20 minutes.

MAKES 12 MUFFINS.

Cheddar Soufflé

6	SLICES WHITE BREAD, CRUSTS REMOVED
1	TABLESPOON LIGHTLY SALTED BUTTER
1	TEASPOON PREPARED MUSTARD
½	POUND SHARP CHEDDAR CHEESE, GRATED (2 CUPS)
6	EGGS
3	CUPS MILK
½	TEASPOON SALT
¼	TEASPOON PAPRIKA

BUTTER a 9 x 13-inch baking dish.

Spread bread with butter and mustard. Cut into 1-inch cubes. Arrange one-half of the bread cubes in the prepared baking dish. Top with Cheddar and the remaining bread cubes.

In a large bowl, beat eggs with milk and salt. Pour over the bread mixture. Sprinkle with paprika. Refrigerate, covered, for at least 3 hours.

Preheat oven to 350 degrees F.

Bake the soufflé until puffed and golden brown, 50 to 60 minutes.

MAKES 8 SERVINGS.

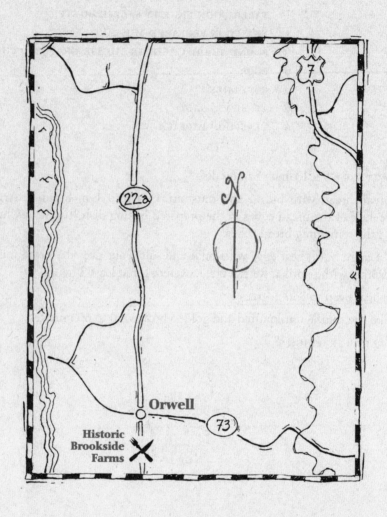

7

22 a

N

Orwell

**Historic
Brookside
Farms**

73

Historic Brookside Farms

P.O. Box 36, Route 22A
Orwell, Vermont 05760
(802) 948-2727

HISTORIC BROOKSIDE FARMS is a family owned and operated inn with a 1790s guesthouse, an 1843 Greek Revival mansion and a gift shop set amidst 300 acres of forest and rolling hills. The mansion and guesthouse, both listed on the National Register of Historic Places, are filled with seventeenth-, eighteenth- and nineteenth-century antiques. Within the mansion, you will find a 10,000-volume library and a formal salon among other common rooms. The Korda family, carrying on five generations of innkeeping, invite you to sample some of their recipes.

NEARBY & NOTEWORTHY: Head west on Route 73 to Mount Independence. The remains of this log-and-earth fort stand as a tribute to the Revolutionary War. Built by the Americans to balance the British Fort Ticonderoga, located directly across Lake Champlain, this fort was at one time home to 10,000 troops.

OUR MENU

Sour Cream Salmon Dip

Cold Cucumber Soup

Grenadine Chicken

Lettuce & Red Cabbage Salad

Sesame Seed Bread

Brandied Sherbet

Sour Cream Salmon Dip

1 CUP SOUR CREAM
1 JAR (2 OUNCES) RED SALMON ROE
½ TEASPOON GARLIC-PARSLEY SALT
½ TEASPOON SEASONED SALT
2 TEASPOONS DRIED SHREDDED GREEN ONION

STIR together sour cream, salmon roe, garlic-parsley salt and seasoned salt. Refrigerate for 1 to 2 hours.

Scoop into a glass dish. Sprinkle with shredded green onion and serve with potato chips or crackers.

MAKES 6 SERVINGS.

Cold Cucumber Soup

2	TABLESPOONS LIGHTLY SALTED BUTTER
3	CUCUMBERS, PEELED, SEEDED AND SLICED
3	TABLESPOONS ALL-PURPOSE FLOUR
3	CUPS CHICKEN STOCK, PREFERABLY HOMEMADE
1	CUP MILK
½	ONION, THINLY SLICED OR CHOPPED
½	CUP HEAVY CREAM
	SALT & GROUND BLACK PEPPER
3	TABLESPOONS SNIPPED FRESH CHIVES OR CHOPPED FRESH TARRAGON

MELT butter in a large heavy saucepan. Add cucumbers and sauté over low heat until tender, about 10 minutes. Puree the cucumber mixture in a food processor or blender. Return to the pan. Add flour and stir until well blended. Gradually whisk in chicken stock.

Pour milk into a small saucepan and add onions. Heat the milk almost to a boil and strain into the chicken stock mixture. Discard the onions. Simmer the soup for 10 minutes. Remove from the heat. Stir in cream and season with salt and pepper to taste. Chill for at least 2 hours before serving.

Serve the soup sprinkled with chives or tarragon.

MAKES 6 SERVINGS.

Grenadine Chicken

1	CUP ALL-PURPOSE FLOUR
¼	CUP GROUND TURMERIC
1	TEASPOON GARLIC SALT
½	TEASPOON SEASONED SALT
½	TEASPOON GROUND BLACK PEPPER
1	CHICKEN (ABOUT 3 POUNDS), CUT INTO 6 PIECES
¼	POUND (1 STICK) LIGHTLY SALTED BUTTER
1	ONION, CHOPPED
1	CAN (7 OUNCES) SLICED MUSHROOMS, DRAINED
2	CUPS GRENADINE
1	CUP BRANDY

PREHEAT oven to 350 degrees F.

In a large sealable plastic bag, combine flour, turmeric, garlic salt, seasoned salt and pepper. Add chicken, a few pieces at a time, and toss to coat well.

Melt butter in a heavy saucepan over medium-high heat. Add the chicken and sauté until lightly browned.

Arrange a layer of chicken in a deep baking dish just large enough to hold the chicken in two layers. Top with one-half of the onions and one-half of the mushrooms. Combine grenadine and brandy. Pour one-half of the grenadine mixture over the chicken. Repeat with the remaining chicken, onions, mushrooms and grenadine mixture.

Cover and bake, basting frequently, until the chicken is very tender and no longer pink inside, about 1 hour.

Serve the chicken over egg noodles with sautéed green beans.

MAKES 6 SERVINGS.

Lettuce & Red Cabbage Salad

½   CUP OLIVE OIL

¼   CUP RED WINE VINEGAR

     SALT & GROUND BLACK PEPPER

1   HEAD ICEBERG LETTUCE, WASHED, DRIED
      AND TORN INTO BITE-SIZE PIECES

¼   HEAD RED CABBAGE, SHREDDED

½   CUCUMBER, SLICED AND CUT INTO QUARTERS

¼   RED ONION, CHOPPED

IN A LARGE salad bowl, whisk together oil and vinegar. Season with salt and pepper to taste. Add lettuce, cabbage, cucumber and onions and toss well.

MAKES 6 SERVINGS.

Sesame Seed Bread

4	CUPS ALL-PURPOSE FLOUR
1	TABLESPOON SALT
2	PACKAGES ACTIVE DRY YEAST
6	TABLESPOONS SUGAR
3	EGGS, LIGHTLY BEATEN
½	CUP VEGETABLE OIL
½-¾	CUP HOT WATER
1	EGG YOLK, WELL BEATEN
2	TABLESPOONS SESAME SEEDS

SIFT flour and salt into a large mixing bowl. Make a well in the flour mixture and sprinkle with yeast and sugar. Add ½ cup lukewarm water and mix until well combined. Cover with a damp cloth and let rise in a warm place for 15 to 30 minutes.

Combine eggs and oil. Add to the flour mixture. Knead on a lightly floured surface, gradually adding hot water as needed, until the dough is smooth and elastic. Cover with a damp cloth and let rise in a warm place until doubled in bulk, about 2 hours.

Preheat oven to 350 degrees F.

Shape the dough into two loaves and place on a baking sheet. Brush with egg yolk and sprinkle with sesame seeds. Bake the loaves until golden brown, 35 to 45 minutes.

MAKES 2 LOAVES.

Brandied Sherbet

6   CUPS RAINBOW SHERBET
¾   CUP BERRY-FLAVORED BRANDY
       FRESH RASPBERRIES OR STRAWBERRIES FOR GARNISH

Scoop sherbet into 6 chilled dessert dishes. Spoon 2 tablespoons of the brandy over each dish and garnish with fresh berries.

MAKES 6 SERVINGS.

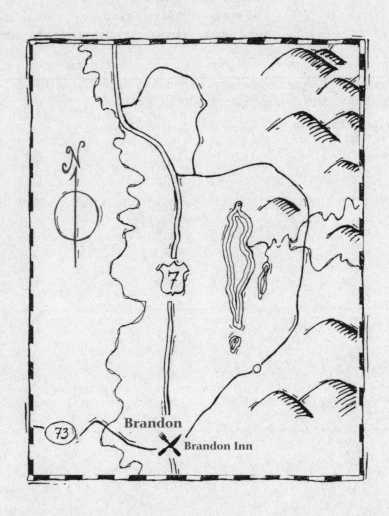

Brandon

✗ Brandon Inn

73

7

Brandon Inn

20 Park Street
Brandon, Vermont 05733
(802) 247-5766

ESTABLISHED IN 1786, Brandon Inn is listed on the National Register of Historic Places. The inn's setting is very picturesque—it faces the Village Green and running east from its doors is a very wide stretch of Park Street, lined with towering maple trees and stately homes. Marble businesses once flourished in the area and, on a stroll along Park Street or nearby Pearl Street, it is easy to imagine the area's prosperity. Guests enjoy award-winning chef Louis Pattis's creations in either of two dining rooms. Weather permitting, lunch and afternoon tea are served on the marble terrace overlooking the expansive lawns.

NEARBY & NOTEWORTHY: Housed in a small barn just behind the inn is the Vermont Ski Museum. Its collection of ski memorabilia and equipment, some of which dates from the turn of the century, highlights how dramatically the industry has changed in less than 100 years.

Seafood Bisque

Smoked Chicken Salad with Walnut Dressing

Lamb Chops with Herbal Cream Sauce

Chocolate Pizza Cookie with Raspberry Sauce

Seafood Bisque

1	10-OUNCE HALIBUT FILLET, CUT INTO 10 PIECES
1	10-OUNCE SALMON FILLET, CUT INTO 10 PIECES
8	LARGE SHRIMP, PEELED AND DEVEINED
	GROUND RED PEPPER
	SALT & GROUND BLACK PEPPER
4	TABLESPOONS UNSALTED BUTTER
3	CELERY STALKS, CUT INTO JULIENNE
1	CARROT, CUT INTO JULIENNE
1	LEEK, WELL WASHED, WHITE PART ONLY, CUT INTO JULIENNE
8	LARGE SEA SCALLOPS, CUT IN HALF
2	CUPS FISH STOCK, PREFERABLY HOMEMADE
½	CUP DRY WHITE WINE
4	CUPS HEAVY CREAM
2	TABLESPOONS SNIPPED FRESH CHIVES

SEASON halibut, salmon and shrimp with red pepper, salt and black pepper to taste.

In a heavy saucepan, melt butter. Add celery, carrots and leeks. Cover the pan and cook the vegetables over low heat until softened but not browned, 1 to 2 minutes. Add the halibut and the shrimp; sauté for 1 minute. Add scallops and the salmon; sauté for 1 minute more. Add fish stock and wine and bring to a boil. Reduce heat and simmer for 2 minutes.

Remove the seafood and the vegetables to a plate and cover loosely with aluminum foil to keep warm. Simmer the bisque until reduced by one-half. Add cream and simmer until reduced by one-third. Season with red pepper, salt and black pepper to taste. Return seafood and vegetables to the bisque and heat over very low heat for 1 minute.

Serve the bisque garnished with chives.

MAKES 8 SERVINGS.

Smoked Chicken Salad with Walnut Dressing

DRESSING

1	CUP WALNUT OIL
⅓	CUP RED WINE VINEGAR
	JUICE OF 2 LEMONS
2	TEASPOONS DIJON MUSTARD
2	TEASPOONS SUGAR
4	SHALLOTS, FINELY CHOPPED
1	CLOVE GARLIC, FINELY CHOPPED
½	TEASPOON CHOPPED FRESH TARRAGON
	SALT & GROUND BLACK PEPPER

SALAD

1	CUCUMBER, PEELED, SEEDED AND CUT INTO JULIENNE, PEEL RESERVED AND CUT INTO JULIENNE
1	TEASPOON SALT PLUS MORE TO TASTE
6	TOMATOES, PEELED, SEEDED AND CUT INTO JULIENNE
2	HEADS BELGIAN ENDIVE, CUT INTO JULIENNE
8	SCALLIONS, CUT TO SAME LENGTH AS CUCUMBER
2	SMOKED CHICKEN BREASTS, BONED, SKINNED AND CUT INTO JULIENNE
	GROUND WHITE PEPPER
	WATERCRESS LEAVES FOR GARNISH
	PEAR SLICES FOR GARNISH

To PREPARE DRESSING: Whisk together oil, vinegar, lemon juice, mustard, sugar, shallots, garlic and tarragon. Season with salt and black pepper to taste.

TO PREPARE SALAD: Place cucumber sticks in a colander. Sprinkle with salt and let stand for 30 minutes. Rinse to remove excess salt. Let dry on paper towels.

Toss the cucumber sticks, cucumber peel, tomatoes, endive, scallions and smoked chicken with the dressing. Season with salt and white pepper to taste.

Serve the salad garnished with watercress leaves and pear slices.

MAKES 8 SERVINGS.

Lamb Chops with Herbal Cream Sauce

¼	POUND (1 STICK) LIGHTLY SALTED BUTTER
16	LOIN LAMB CHOPS, TRIMMED, LEAVING ONLY THE EYE OF THE MEAT ON THE BONE
4	CLOVES GARLIC, CRUSHED
	SALT & GROUND BLACK PEPPER
6	SHALLOTS, FINELY CHOPPED
½	CUP LAMB OR VEGETABLE STOCK, PREFERABLY HOMEMADE
1	CUP HEAVY CREAM
1	TABLESPOON FINELY CHOPPED FRESH PARSLEY
2	TEASPOONS FINELY CHOPPED FRESH ROSEMARY
2	TEASPOONS FINELY CHOPPED FRESH THYME
	FRESH HERB SPRIGS FOR GARNISH

MELT 4 tablespoons of the butter in a large heavy skillet. Add lamb and sauté until browned on the outside and light pink in the center, about 3 minutes. Add garlic and season with salt and pepper to taste. Remove the lamb to a plate and cover loosely with aluminum foil to keep warm.

Add shallots to the skillet. Cover and cook over low heat until transparent, 2 to 3 minutes. Stir in lamb or vegetable stock and simmer until reduced by one-half. Add cream and simmer until reduced by one-half. Add the remaining 4 tablespoons butter, parsley, rosemary and thyme. Gently shake the skillet as the butter melts. Season with salt and pepper to taste.

Pour the sauce over the chops and garnish with fresh herbs. Serve the lamb with roasted red potatoes and green beans.

MAKES 8 SERVINGS.

Chocolate Pizza Cookie with Raspberry Sauce

½	POUND (2 STICKS) UNSALTED BUTTER
½	CUP SUGAR
½	CUP PACKED DARK BROWN SUGAR
1	EGG, LIGHTLY BEATEN
½	TEASPOON PURE VANILLA EXTRACT
1¼	CUPS ALL-PURPOSE FLOUR
½	TEASPOON BAKING SODA
½	TEASPOON SALT
9	OUNCES CHOCOLATE CHIPS
3	OUNCES BUTTERSCOTCH CHIPS
1	CUP FRESH OR FROZEN RASPBERRIES
1	TABLESPOON FRESH LEMON JUICE

PREHEAT oven to 350 degrees F.

Cream butter, 6 tablespoons of the sugar and brown sugar. Beat in egg and vanilla. Stir in flour, baking soda and salt. Stir in 6 ounces of the chocolate chips.

Press the dough into an 8-inch pie pan. Bake the cookie until golden and still soft to the touch, about 25 minutes.

Sprinkle the remaining 3 ounces chocolate chips and butterscotch chips over the hot cookie. Let melt and spread to form an icing. Let cool for 10 minutes.

Before serving, puree raspberries, the remaining 2 tablespoons sugar and lemon juice in a blender.

Slice the cookie as you would a pie and serve topped with the pureed raspberries.

MAKES ONE 8-INCH COOKIE.

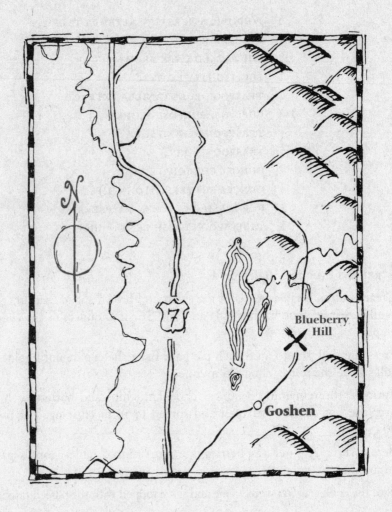

Blueberry
Hill

Goshen

7

N

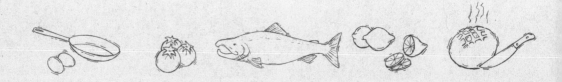

Blueberry Hill

Goshen, Vermont 05733
(802) 247-6735/(800) 448-0707

BLUEBERRY HILL is located on a country road in the small town of Goshen, population 300. Situated in the heart of Addison County's very best cross-country ski area, this inn draws skiers all winter and hikers and environmental enthusiasts throughout the year. Years ago, Blueberry Hill was an Addison County hill farm. Now it is a place to enjoy comfortable accommodations and fine cuisine with owner Tony Clark presiding over the table.

NEARBY & NOTEWORTHY: The National Forest Service maintains a blueberry-picking area on a nearby hillside. If you would like to venture a little farther, only a few miles away is Silver Lake, a national forest campground with a picnic area and hiking trails.

Cornmeal–Crusted Goat Cheese Salad

Honey Oatmeal Sesame Bread

Grilled Swordfish with Pacific Marinade

Lemon Kiwi Tart

Cornmeal–Crusted Goat Cheese Salad

DRESSING
½   CUP HEAVY CREAM
¼   CUP DIJON MUSTARD
4   TEASPOONS RED WINE VINEGAR
  SALT & GROUND BLACK PEPPER

GOAT CHEESE & SALAD
2   CYLINDRICAL PACKAGES (4 OUNCES EACH) GOAT CHEESE
2   EGGS, BEATEN
½   CUP MILK
1   CUP CORNMEAL
  SALT & GROUND BLACK PEPPER
½   CUP ALL–PURPOSE FLOUR
  CANOLA OIL FOR FRYING
6   CUPS WASHED AND DRIED MESCLUN (ARUGULA, CHERVIL, GREEN OAK LEAF LETTUCE, LOLLO ROSSA, MÂCHE, MIZUNA, RED OAK LEAF LETTUCE, TAT–SOI)
  WALNUT HALVES FOR GARNISH

TO PREPARE DRESSING: Whisk together cream, mustard and vinegar. Season with salt and pepper to taste.

TO PREPARE GOAT CHEESE: Slice goat cheese into ¼-inch-thick rounds. Beat eggs and milk until well combined. In another bowl, season cornmeal with salt and pepper to taste. Dip each goat cheese slice in flour, then the egg mixture and finally the cornmeal. (Coat each slice well.)

Pour 1 inch of oil into a large, deep heavy skillet. Heat until the oil registers 350 degrees F on a deep-frying thermometer. Fry goat cheese until golden brown, about 45 seconds. Remove to a plate and cover with aluminum foil to keep warm.

TO PREPARE SALAD: Distribute mesclun evenly among 6 plates. Arrange 3 goat cheese rounds on each plate and garnish with walnut halves. Drizzle the dressing over the salad.

MAKES 6 SERVINGS.

Honey Oatmeal Sesame Bread

1	CUP OLD-FASHIONED ROLLED OATS
¾	CUP SESAME SEEDS
4	TABLESPOONS LIGHTLY SALTED BUTTER
1	CUP BOILING WATER
1	CUP HONEY
2	TEASPOONS SALT
2	PACKAGES ACTIVE DRY YEAST
1	TEASPOON SUGAR
1	CUP WHOLE WHEAT FLOUR
8	CUPS UNBLEACHED ALL-PURPOSE FLOUR PLUS ADDITIONAL AS NEEDED

COMBINE oats, sesame seeds, butter and boiling water in a large bowl. Stir to melt butter. Add 1 cup cold water, honey and salt. Stir until combined. Let cool to lukewarm.

Meanwhile, combine yeast with ½ cup lukewarm water in a large bowl. Sprinkle with sugar to help activate the yeast and let stand until the mixture is bubbly, 5 to 8 minutes.

Stir the oat mixture and whole wheat flour into the yeast mixture. Blend in as much unbleached flour as possible. Knead on a lightly floured surface until the dough is smooth and elastic, incorporating more of the flour as needed until it is no longer sticky. Place the dough in a large oiled bowl. Cover with a damp cloth and let rise in a warm place until doubled in bulk, 1 to 2 hours.

Lightly oil three loaf pans. Divide the dough evenly among the prepared pans. Cover and let rise again in a warm place until doubled in bulk.

Preheat oven to 375 degrees F.

Bake the loaves until golden brown, about 45 minutes.

MAKES 3 LOAVES.

Grilled Swordfish with Pacific Marinade

The swordfish is best when allowed to marinate for up to 4 hours.
If you marinate it any longer, however, the fish will seem dry after grilling.

1	CUP RED WINE VINEGAR
½	CUP LIGHT SOY SAUCE
½	CUP SESAME OIL
¼	CUP HONEY
3	TABLESPOONS ORANGE JUICE
2	TEASPOONS CHINESE CHILI SAUCE (AVAILABLE AT SPECIALTY FOOD SHOPS)
1	TEASPOON RED PEPPER FLAKES
1	LARGE RED ONION, CHOPPED
¼	CUP FINELY CHOPPED FRESH GINGER
4	CLOVES GARLIC, CHOPPED
	GRATED ZEST OF 1 ORANGE
6	4-OUNCE SWORDFISH STEAKS

WHISK together vinegar, soy sauce, oil, honey, orange juice, chili sauce and red pepper flakes. Stir in onions, ginger, garlic and 1 tablespoon of the orange zest. Let stand for 30 minutes.

Marinate swordfish in the mixture for at least 1 hour but no longer than 4 hours.

Prepare a grill.

Grill the swordfish until it is opaque in the center, 2 to 3 minutes each side. Garnish with the remaining orange zest and serve with couscous and grilled vegetables.

MAKES 6 SERVINGS.

Lemon Kiwi Tart

Tart Shell
¼	POUND (1 STICK) UNSALTED BUTTER
½	CUP ALL-PURPOSE FLOUR
2	TABLESPOONS SUGAR
	PINCH OF SALT

Lemon Curd
6	TABLESPOONS UNSALTED BUTTER
1	CUP SUGAR
⅓	CUP LEMON JUICE
4	EGGS, LIGHTLY BEATEN
	GRATED ZEST OF 1½ LEMONS

2	KIWIS, PEELED AND THINLY SLICED
3	STRAWBERRIES FOR GARNISH
	FRESH MINT SPRIGS FOR GARNISH

To PREPARE TART SHELL: Preheat oven to 375 degrees F.

Mix butter, flour, sugar and salt with a mixer set at low speed until the dough is crumbly. Add 1 tablespoon cold water and mix at high speed until the dough forms into a ball.

Roll out the dough and press into an 8-inch tart pan. Line the tart shell with aluminum foil and weight with beans. Bake the tart shell until golden brown, 10 to 12 minutes. Remove the beans and foil. Let the tart shell cool for 15 minutes before removing from the pan.

TO PREPARE LEMON CURD: Melt butter in a saucepan over medium-high heat. Add sugar and lemon juice and stir until the sugar is dissolved. Add eggs and whisk continuously until the mixture comes to a rolling boil. Pour into a bowl and stir in lemon zest. Cover and let cool completely in the refrigerator.

TO ASSEMBLE TART: Fill the tart shell with lemon curd. Arrange kiwi slices over the top and garnish with strawberries and mint.

MAKES ONE 8-INCH TART.

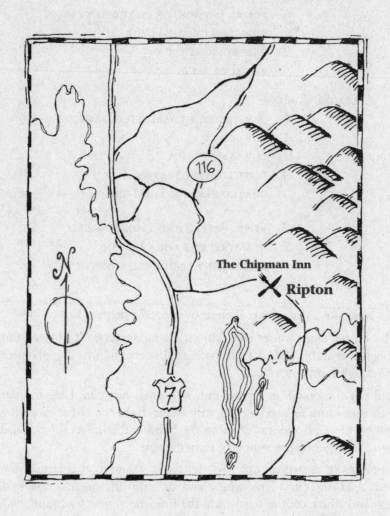

The Chipman Inn

✗ Ripton

116

7

The Chipman Inn

Route 125
Ripton, Vermont 05766
(802) 388-2390/(800) 890-2390

THIS TRADITIONAL country inn, built in 1828, is located in the small village of Ripton and surrounded by the Green Mountain National Forest. As your eye travels along the stone-walled fields, into the dense forest and up to the impressive vista of Breadloaf Mountain and the Green Mountain Range, you will come to understand where Robert Frost, a summer resident of the town, drew his inspiration from. Guests can relax in front of the fire in the comfortable sitting room and bar or in the sunny reading room. The following menu is a sample of what guests enjoy in the candlelit dining room.

NEARBY & NOTEWORTHY: A one-mile drive east on Route 125 will lead you to the Robert Frost Interpretive Trail. A gravel path winds through mature forest and small clearings and along a trickling stream. Poems by Frost are displayed on small posts along this ½-mile walk. Just east of the trailhead on Route 125 is the Robert Frost Picnic Area, and just beyond this is a dirt road that leads to Frost's summer cabin.

Cheese Olives

Salmon Spread

Dilled Zucchini Soup

Green Bean Salad with Tuna Sauce

Veal Marengo

Lemon–Almond Pound Cake

Cheese Olives

½   POUND SHARP CHEDDAR CHEESE, GRATED (2 CUPS)
¼   POUND (1 STICK) LIGHTLY SALTED BUTTER
1   CUP ALL-PURPOSE FLOUR
1   TEASPOON PAPRIKA
¼   TEASPOON TABASCO SAUCE
36 PIMIENTO-STUFFED GREEN OLIVES

PREHEAT oven to 375 degrees F.

In a food processor, mix Cheddar, butter, flour, paprika and Tabasco until a dough begins to form, 1 to 2 minutes.

Wrap about 1 teaspoon of the dough around each olive and set on a baking sheet. Bake the olives until golden brown and crisp, about 20 minutes.

MAKES 6 SERVINGS.

Salmon Spread

4	OUNCES CREAM CHEESE
1½	TEASPOONS LEMON JUICE
1	TEASPOON BOTTLED HORSERADISH
¾	TEASPOON WORCESTERSHIRE SAUCE
¼	TEASPOON TABASCO SAUCE
⅛	TEASPOON SALT
	PINCH OF GROUND WHITE PEPPER
¼	TEASPOON NATURAL HICKORY SEASONING
1	CAN (7.5 OUNCES) RED SALMON, DRAINED
¼	CUP CHOPPED WALNUTS (OPTIONAL)
¼	CUP CHOPPED FRESH PARSLEY (OPTIONAL)

BLEND cream cheese, lemon juice, horseradish, Worcestershire, Tabasco, salt, pepper and hickory seasoning. Add salmon and stir until just combined.

Serve immediately with crackers or form into a ball and chill for 1 hour. Roll the chilled ball in walnuts and parsley before serving.

MAKES 6 SERVINGS.

Dilled Zucchini Soup

1   TABLESPOON LIGHTLY SALTED BUTTER

3   SMALL ZUCCHINI (ABOUT 1 POUND), SLICED

3   SMALL YELLOW SQUASH (ABOUT 1 POUND), SLICED

1   SMALL LEEK, WELL WASHED, WHITE PART ONLY, THINLY SLICED

4   CUPS CHICKEN STOCK, PREFERABLY HOMEMADE

1   TABLESPOON CHOPPED FRESH DILL PLUS ADDITIONAL FOR GARNISH

1   TEASPOON DILL SEEDS

MELT butter in a large pot. Sauté zucchini, yellow squash and leeks over low heat until softened, about 10 minutes. Add chicken stock and bring to a boil.

Meanwhile, wrap fresh dill and dill seeds in several layers of cheesecloth; tie with string to secure. Add to the soup and boil until the squash is tender, 15 to 20 minutes.

Discard the cheesecloth pouch. Serve the soup garnished with fresh dill.

MAKES 6 SERVINGS.

Green Bean Salad with Tuna Sauce

Top this salad with cherry tomatoes, black olives and sliced hard-boiled eggs for an interesting variation.

1	POUND SMALL RED POTATOES
1	POUND GREEN BEANS, TRIMMED
3	OUNCES (FROM A 6-OUNCE CAN) SOLID WHITE TUNA, PACKED IN OIL
	JUICE OF ½ LEMON
1	EGG YOLK, AT ROOM TEMPERATURE
2	CLOVES GARLIC, CRUSHED
¼	TEASPOON SALT
⅛	TEASPOON GROUND RED PEPPER
¼	CUP OLIVE OIL
¼	CUP VEGETABLE OIL
	RED LETTUCE LEAVES, WASHED AND DRIED

BOIL potatoes in salted water to cover until tender, 10 to 15 minutes. Drain and slice into ¼-inch-thick rounds when cool enough to handle.

Meanwhile, boil green beans in salted water to cover until tender, about 5 minutes. Plunge into cold water and pat dry.

In a blender or food processor, puree tuna, lemon juice, egg yolk, garlic, salt and red pepper. With the motor running, add olive oil and vegetable oil in a steady stream. Blend until just incorporated.

Arrange lettuce leaves on a platter and top with the potatoes and the green beans. Drizzle the sauce over the salad.

MAKES 6 SERVINGS.

Veal Marengo

2-3	TABLESPOONS OLIVE OIL
3	POUNDS VEAL SHOULDER OR LEG, TRIMMED AND CUT INTO 2-INCH CUBES
1½	CUPS FINELY CHOPPED ONIONS (ABOUT 2 MEDIUM)
2	CUPS DRY WHITE WINE
3	TABLESPOONS ALL-PURPOSE FLOUR
1	TEASPOON SALT
¼	TEASPOON GROUND BLACK PEPPER
2	MEDIUM TOMATOES, PEELED, SEEDED AND CHOPPED (1 CUP)
1	CLOVE GARLIC, CRUSHED
1	TEASPOON DRIED BASIL
1	TEASPOON DRIED THYME LEAVES
2	BAY LEAVES
1	POUND MUSHROOMS, TRIMMED AND CUT IN HALVES OR QUARTERS
	CHOPPED FRESH PARSLEY FOR GARNISH

ARRANGE an oven rack in the lowest position. Preheat oven to 325 degrees F.

Heat 2 tablespoons of the oil in a heavy skillet over medium-high heat. Brown veal in batches and transfer to a Dutch oven. Lower the heat and add the remaining 1 tablespoon oil, if necessary. Add onions and sauté until translucent, about 4 minutes. Add wine and bring to a boil, scraping up the brown bits from the bottom and sides of the skillet. Remove from the heat.

Set the Dutch oven over low heat. Add flour, salt and pepper. Cook, stirring, for 3 to 4 minutes. Stir in the onion mixture, tomatoes, garlic, basil, thyme and bay leaves. Bring to a boil. Cover, place in the oven and bake the stew for 1 hour.

Stir in mushrooms and bake the stew for 20 minutes more. (If the sauce is too thin, simmer over medium heat until reduced to the desired consistency.) Discard the bay leaves.

Garnish the veal with parsley and serve over egg noodles.

MAKES 6 SERVINGS.

Lemon–Almond Pound Cake

Pound Cake

1	CUP BLANCHED ALMONDS
1	CUP SUGAR
½	POUND (2 STICKS) LIGHTLY SALTED BUTTER, AT ROOM TEMPERATURE
4	EGGS
	GRATED ZEST OF 1 LEMON
1	CUP ALL-PURPOSE FLOUR
1	TEASPOON BAKING POWDER
⅓	CUP LEMON JUICE

Glaze

2	CUPS CONFECTIONERS' SUGAR
¼	CUP LEMON JUICE

To prepare pound cake: Preheat oven to 350 degrees F. Lightly butter and flour an 8-inch round baking dish that is at least 2 inches deep.

Process almonds and sugar in a food processor until the almonds are finely ground. In a large bowl, cream butter. Add the almond mixture and beat with an electric mixer for 3 minutes. Add eggs, one at a time, beating well after each addition. Stir in lemon zest.

Sift flour and baking powder into another bowl. Beat one-half of the flour mixture into the almond mixture. Beat in lemon juice, then beat in the remaining flour mixture.

Pour the batter into the prepared pan. Bake the cake until a tester comes out clean, about 55 minutes.

TO PREPARE GLAZE: Whisk confectioners' sugar and lemon juice until smooth. Pour over the cooled cake and let stand for 1 hour before serving for the glaze to set.

MAKES ONE 8-INCH CAKE.

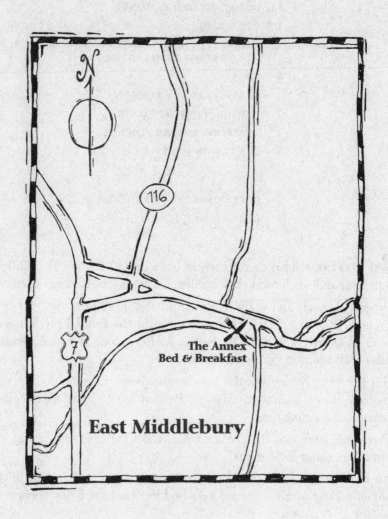

**The Annex
Bed & Breakfast**

East Middlebury

The Annex
Bed & Breakfast

Route 125
East Middlebury, Vermont 05740
(802) 388-3233

THE ANNEX is located at the foot of the Green Mountains in the quaint hamlet of East Middlebury. This 1800s home, located on the old stagecoach route, has six comfortable rooms, all with quilts handmade by the owner. While breakfast is served, there is often lively conversation and discussion of area lore.

NEARBY & NOTEWORTHY: For those who want to discover the Green Mountain National Forest, hike along part of the Long Trail, which stretches from Massachusetts to Canada. Drive to the top of Middlebury Gap on Route 125, where signs mark the trail crossing.

Fruit Muffins

Banana Oatmeal Muffins

Granola

Breakfast Casserole

Popovers

Johnny Cake

Fruit Muffins

Raspberries are especially good in this recipe, but any fruit can be used.

3	CUPS PLUS ½ TEASPOON ALL-PURPOSE FLOUR
1	CUP SUGAR
4	TEASPOONS BAKING POWDER
2	EGGS, WELL BEATEN
1	CUP MILK
½	CUP VEGETABLE OIL
2	CUPS FROZEN FRUIT (RASPBERRIES, BLUEBERRIES, PEACHES)

PREHEAT oven to 400 degrees F. Lightly oil a 12-cup muffin tin.

Combine 3 cups of the flour, sugar and baking powder. Add eggs, milk and oil. Stir until just combined. (The batter will be lumpy.) Dust fruit with the remaining ½ teaspoon flour and gently fold into the batter.

Divide the batter evenly among the prepared muffin cups. Bake the muffins until golden brown and a tester comes out clean, 20 to 25 minutes.

MAKES 12 MUFFINS.

Banana Oatmeal Muffins

1½	CUPS ALL-PURPOSE FLOUR
1	CUP QUICK-COOKING ROLLED OATS
½	CUP SUGAR
2	TEASPOONS BAKING POWDER
1	TEASPOON BAKING SODA
½	TEASPOON SALT
1	EGG, WELL BEATEN
¾	CUP MILK
⅔	CUP MASHED VERY RIPE BANANAS
⅓	CUP VEGETABLE OIL

PREHEAT oven to 400 degrees F. Lightly grease a 12-cup muffin tin.

Combine flour, oats, sugar, baking powder, baking soda and salt. Add egg, milk, bananas and oil. Mix well.

Divide the batter evenly among the prepared muffin cups. Bake the muffins until golden brown and a tester comes out clean, 18 to 20 minutes.

MAKES 12 MUFFINS.

Granola

4 CUPS OLD-FASHIONED ROLLED OATS
2 CUPS RAW WHEAT GERM
1 CUP SWEETENED FLAKED COCONUT
1 CUP CHOPPED WALNUTS
¾ CUP PACKED LIGHT BROWN SUGAR
¾ CUP VEGETABLE OIL
2 TABLESPOONS PURE VANILLA EXTRACT

PREHEAT oven to 350 degrees F.

Combine oats, wheat germ, coconut, walnuts and brown sugar. Add oil, ⅓ cup lukewarm water and vanilla. Mix well.

Spread evenly in a large shallow baking dish. Bake the granola, stirring frequently, until golden brown, about 1 hour.

Serve the granola with milk or yogurt or add to pancake batter or cookie dough.

MAKES 8 TO 12 SERVINGS.

Breakfast Casserole

12   SLICES WHITE BREAD, CRUSTS
        REMOVED, CUBED

½   POUND SHARP CHEDDAR CHEESE,
        GRATED (2 CUPS)

½   POUND HAM, FINELY CHOPPED

6   EGGS, LIGHTLY BEATEN

3   CUPS MILK

1   TEASPOON DRY MUSTARD

1   TEASPOON SALT

4   TABLESPOONS LIGHTLY SALTED
        BUTTER, MELTED

PREHEAT oven to 350 degrees F. Lightly butter a large baking dish. Arrange bread in the prepared dish. Top with Cheddar and ham.

Beat eggs with milk, mustard and salt. Pour over the bread mixture and top with melted butter.

Bake the casserole until puffed and golden brown, 50 to 60 minutes.

MAKES 6 SERVINGS.

Popovers

2	EGGS
¾	CUP PLUS 2 TABLESPOONS MILK
¼	POUND (1 STICK) LIGHTLY SALTED BUTTER, MELTED
1	CUP ALL-PURPOSE FLOUR
¼	TEASPOON SALT

BUTTER 6 ramekins.

In a blender, mix eggs for no more than 5 seconds at low speed. Add milk, melted butter, flour and salt. Blend until well combined.

Divide the batter evenly among the prepared ramekins. Arrange on a baking sheet and place in a cold oven. Set the oven at 400 degrees F. Bake the popovers until puffed and golden brown, about 50 minutes.

MAKES 6 POPOVERS.

Johnny Cake

1	CUP ALL-PURPOSE FLOUR
1	CUP CORNMEAL
½	CUP SUGAR
1	TEASPOON BAKING SODA
1	TEASPOON BAKING POWDER
1	TEASPOON SALT
1	EGG, LIGHTLY BEATEN
1½	CUPS SOUR MILK OR BUTTERMILK

PREHEAT oven to 425 degrees F. Lightly oil an 8-inch square baking dish.

Combine flour, cornmeal, sugar, baking soda, baking powder and salt. Beat in egg and sour milk or buttermilk.

Pour into the prepared pan. Bake the cake until golden brown and a tester comes out clean, about 25 minutes.

MAKES ONE 8-INCH CAKE.

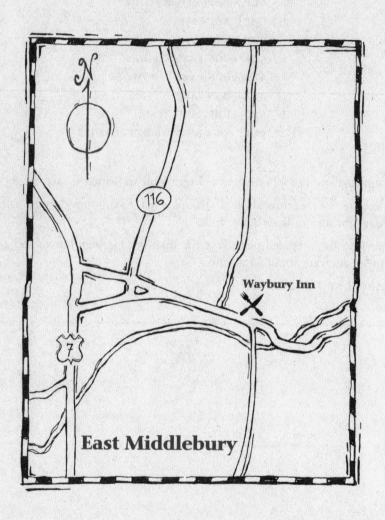

116

Waybury Inn

7

East Middlebury

Waybury Inn

Route 125
East Middlebury, Vermont 05740
(802) 388-4015/(800) 348-1810

WAYBURY INN was built in 1810 as a stagecoach stop on the east-west passage through the Green Mountains. Stagecoaches would set off from Hancock, on the county's eastern border. After a long climb to the town of Ripton and a descent into East Middlebury, the stagecoach would leave passengers at the inn for rest and refreshments. Waybury Inn has been in continuous operation ever since, and it still offers good country fare to all those who pass through its doors.

NEARBY & NOTEWORTHY: Trace the route of the old stagecoaches—drive east on Route 125 through the Green Mountain National Forest to Ripton and Hancock. Along the way you will pass Middlebury College's Breadloaf campus—the site of the college's summer school graduate English program as well as of the nationally acclaimed Breadloaf Writer's Conference.

Kidney Bean Relish

Carrot–Ginger Soup

Green Salad with Dried Fruits & Maple Vinaigrette

Grilled Swordfish with Mango Salsa

Sugar Snap Peas with Butter & Chive Blossoms

Chocolate Hearts of Cream with Raspberry Glaze

Kidney Bean Relish

3   CELERY STALKS, CHOPPED
1   SMALL ONION, CHOPPED
2   HARD-BOILED EGGS, CHOPPED
1   CAN (15 OUNCES) KIDNEY BEANS,
      DRAINED AND RINSED
1   TABLESPOON MAYONNAISE
2   TEASPOONS DILL RELISH
1   TEASPOON CURRY POWDER
½   TEASPOON SALT
¼   TEASPOON GROUND WHITE PEPPER

COMBINE celery, onions and eggs. Add beans, mayonnaise, relish, curry powder, salt and pepper. Mix well. Chill for at least 1 hour before serving.

Serve the relish with crackers.

MAKES 8 SERVINGS.

Carrot–Ginger Soup

3	TABLESPOONS OLIVE OIL
1	CUP CHOPPED ONIONS
3	TABLESPOONS CHOPPED FRESH GINGER
3	CLOVES GARLIC, FINELY CHOPPED
10	LARGE CARROTS, PEELED AND CUT INTO 1-INCH-THICK SLICES
8	CUPS CHICKEN OR VEGETABLE STOCK, PREFERABLY HOMEMADE
	SALT & GROUND WHITE PEPPER
¼	CUP CHOPPED FRESH PARSLEY

HEAT oil in a large pot over low heat. Add onions, ginger and garlic and sauté until the onions are translucent, about 5 minutes. Add carrots and chicken or vegetable stock. Simmer until the carrots are tender, about 30 minutes.

Puree the soup in a food processor or blender, in batches if necessary. Season with salt and pepper to taste.

Serve the soup garnished with parsley.

MAKES 8 SERVINGS.

Green Salad with Dried Fruits & Maple Vinaigrette

VINAIGRETTE

1	CUP OLIVE OIL
½	CUP VEGETABLE OIL
6	TABLESPOONS PURE MAPLE SYRUP
¼	CUP BALSAMIC VINEGAR
2	TABLESPOONS CHOPPED FRESH PARSLEY
1½	CLOVES GARLIC, FINELY CHOPPED
	SALT & FRESHLY GROUND BLACK PEPPER

SALAD

1	HEAD GREEN LEAF LETTUCE, WASHED, DRIED AND TORN INTO BITE-SIZE PIECES
1	HEAD RED LEAF LETTUCE, WASHED, DRIED AND TORN INTO BITE-SIZE PIECES
4	CUPS WASHED AND DRIED MESCLUN (ARUGULA, CHERVIL, GREEN OAK LEAF LETTUCE, LOLLO ROSSA, MÂCHE, MIZUNA, RED OAK LEAF LETTUCE, TAT-SOI)
½	CUP DRIED CRANBERRIES
½	CUP DRIED APRICOTS, CUT INTO ¼-INCH-THICK SLICES
½	CUP WALNUTS, TOASTED AND CHOPPED

TO PREPARE VINAIGRETTE: In a bowl, stir together olive oil and vegetable oil. Combine maple syrup and vinegar in a blender. With the motor running, slowly add the oil mixture and blend until well combined. Stir in parsley and garlic. Season with salt and pepper to taste.

TO PREPARE SALAD: In a large bowl, toss together lettuces, cranberries, apricots and the vinaigrette. Top with toasted walnuts.

MAKES 8 SERVINGS.

Grilled Swordfish with Mango Salsa

Mango Salsa

3	RIPE MANGOES, CUBED
1	LARGE RED BELL PEPPER, CHOPPED
½	CUP CHOPPED SCALLIONS
¼	CUP CHOPPED FRESH CILANTRO
1	FRESH JALAPEÑO OR SERRANO PEPPER, SEEDED AND FINELY CHOPPED
3	CLOVES GARLIC, FINELY CHOPPED
	JUICE OF 1 LEMON
2	TABLESPOONS FRESH ORANGE JUICE
	SALT & GROUND BLACK PEPPER

Swordfish & Marinade

¼	CUP OLIVE OIL
	JUICE OF 2 LIMES
8	10-OUNCE SWORDFISH STEAKS

To prepare mango salsa: Mix together mangoes, bell peppers, scallions, cilantro, jalapeño or serrano peppers, garlic, lemon juice and orange juice. Season with salt and pepper to taste. Chill for at least 1 hour before serving.

TO PREPARE SWORDFISH & MARINADE: Prepare a grill.

In a small bowl, combine oil and lime juice. Brush swordfish with the oil mixture. Grill the swordfish, turning once and basting again with the oil mixture, until it is opaque in the center, about 5 minutes each side.

Top the swordfish with the mango salsa and serve with rice pilaf.

MAKES 8 SERVINGS.

Sugar Snap Peas with Butter & Chive Blossoms

2   POUNDS SUGAR SNAP PEAS, STEMS AND
    STRINGS REMOVED
1   TABLESPOON LIGHTLY SALTED BUTTER
12 CHIVE BLOSSOMS, PLUCKED APART OR
    1 TABLESPOON FRESH SNIPPED CHIVES
    SALT & FRESHLY GROUND BLACK PEPPER

BOIL snap peas in salted water to cover for 1 minute. Plunge into cold water to stop cooking. Drain well.

Toss the snap peas with butter and chive blossoms or chives. Season with salt and pepper to taste.

MAKES 8 SERVINGS.

Chocolate Hearts of Cream with Raspberry Glaze

RASPBERRY GLAZE

½ CUP SEEDLESS RASPBERRY PRESERVES

2 TABLESPOONS CHAMBORD OR WATER

CHOCOLATE CREAM

1½ POUNDS (THREE 8-OUNCE PACKAGES) CREAM CHEESE, AT ROOM TEMPERATURE

1 CUP SUGAR

½ CUP UNSWEETENED COCOA POWDER

3 TABLESPOONS CHAMBORD

2 CUPS HEAVY CREAM

1 PINT RASPBERRIES

TO PREPARE RASPBERRY GLAZE: In a small saucepan, cook raspberry preserves and Chambord or water over low heat, stirring constantly until smooth. Let cool to room temperature.

TO PREPARE CHOCOLATE CREAM: Combine cream cheese, sugar and cocoa powder in a large bowl and mix until smooth. Stir in Chambord.

In another bowl, whip cream until stiff peaks begin to form. Fold into the cream cheese mixture.

Scoop or use a pastry bag to pipe the chocolate cream into 8 dishes. Top with the raspberry glaze and fresh raspberries.

MAKES 8 SERVINGS.

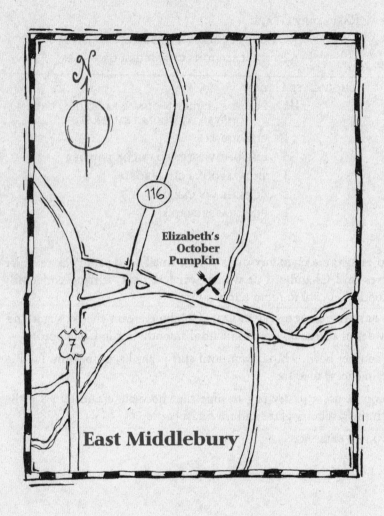

N

116

**Elizabeth's
October
Pumpkin**

✗

7

East Middlebury

Elizabeth's October Pumpkin

P.O. Box 226, Route 125
East Middlebury, Vermont 05740
(802) 388-9525

ELIZABETH'S OCTOBER PUMPKIN is located at the foot of Middlebury Gap, in the heart of Robert Frost country. This Greek Revival home—now painted a striking pumpkin color—was built in 1850. The house was updated in the early 1980s and has four guest rooms, all with country quilts. The following recipes have brought rave reviews from guests over the years.

NEARBY & NOTEWORTHY: Just a short drive south is Lake Dunmore, one of Vermont's largest lakes. Branbury State Park, located along Lake Dunmore's shores, has a sandy beach and picnic areas. From the campground, hike to the unusual Falls of Llana and to the peak of Mount Moosalamoo. The view of the lake from Moosalamoo's Rattlesnake Point is spectacular.

Fruit Shake

Fresh Fruit Platter with Ginger Cream

Seafood Brunch Bake

Sour Cream Coffeecake with Nut Topping

Fruit Shake

4	CUPS FRESH STRAWBERRIES OR RASPBERRIES
1⅓	CUPS NONFAT DRY MILK
1	CUP PLAIN LOW-FAT YOGURT
1	CUP ICE CUBES
¼	CUP SUGAR
1	TEASPOON PURE VANILLA EXTRACT

IN A BLENDER, combine strawberries, dry milk, yogurt, ice cubes, 1 cup water, sugar and vanilla. Blend until the ice is crushed. Serve immediately.

MAKES 6 SERVINGS.

Fresh Fruit Platter with Ginger Cream

Prepare the ginger cream the night before so assembly in the morning is effortless.

1	CUP LOW-FAT SOUR CREAM
2	TABLESPOONS ORANGE JUICE CONCENTRATE, THAWED
2	TABLESPOONS PACKED DARK BROWN SUGAR
½	TEASPOON GROUND GINGER
⅛	TEASPOON GROUND NUTMEG
6	CUPS SLICED SEASONAL FRUITS (MELONS, BERRIES, KIWIS, APPLES, GRAPES)

IN A SMALL bowl, whisk together sour cream, juice concentrate, brown sugar, ginger and nutmeg. Cover and refrigerate for at least 1 hour or overnight.

Arrange fruits on a platter or individual plates. Serve the sauce alongside to drizzle over the fruits.

MAKES 6 SERVINGS.

Seafood Brunch Bake

2	TABLESPOONS LIGHTLY SALTED BUTTER
½	POUND MUSHROOMS, TRIMMED AND SLICED
¾	POUND FRESH OR FROZEN LUMP CRABMEAT, SQUEEZED DRY
⅔	CUP SLICED SCALLIONS
6	CUPS CUBED FRENCH BREAD
½	POUND GRUYÈRE CHEESE, GRATED (2 CUPS)
4	EGGS, WELL BEATEN
2½	CUPS MILK
1	TEASPOON DRY MUSTARD
¾	TEASPOON SALT
½	TEASPOON GROUND NUTMEG
¼	TEASPOON GROUND BLACK PEPPER
¼	TEASPOON TABASCO SAUCE

LIGHTLY butter a large shallow baking dish.

Melt butter in a skillet over medium-high heat. Add mushrooms and cook, stirring occasionally, until browned, about 8 minutes. Remove from the heat. Stir in crabmeat and scallions.

Pressing the layers down gently as you go, spread one-half of the bread cubes in the baking dish, top with one-half of the crabmeat mixture and sprinkle with one-half of the Gruyère. Repeat with the remaining bread, crabmeat mixture and Gruyère.

In a large bowl, whisk eggs, milk and dry mustard until the mustard is dissolved. Add salt, nutmeg, black pepper and Tabasco and whisk until well blended. Pour the egg mixture over the casserole. Refrigerate, covered, for at least 4 hours.

Preheat oven to 350 degrees F.

Bake the casserole until puffed and golden brown, 40 to 50 minutes.

MAKES 6 SERVINGS.

Sour Cream Coffeecake with Nut Topping

NUT TOPPING

1¼	CUPS CHOPPED WALNUTS OR PECANS
¼	CUP SUGAR
1	TABLESPOON GROUND CINNAMON

COFFEECAKE

½	POUND (2 STICKS) LIGHTLY SALTED BUTTER, AT ROOM TEMPERATURE
1¼	CUPS SUGAR
2	EGGS, LIGHTLY BEATEN
1	CUP LOW-FAT SOUR CREAM
1	TEASPOON PURE VANILLA EXTRACT
2	CUPS ALL-PURPOSE FLOUR
1	TEASPOON BAKING POWDER
½	TEASPOON BAKING SODA
½	TEASPOON SALT

TO PREPARE NUT TOPPING: Combine walnuts or pecans, sugar and cinnamon.

TO PREPARE COFFEECAKE: Preheat oven to 350 degrees F. Lightly butter a 9-inch tube pan.

In a large bowl, cream butter and sugar. Beat in eggs, sour cream and vanilla. Mix together flour, baking powder, baking soda and salt. Gradually stir into the sugar mixture until just combined.

Spread one-half of the nut topping in the bottom of the pan. Pour one-half of the batter over the nut topping. Repeat with the remaining nut topping and batter. Bake the coffeecake until golden brown and a tester comes out clean, 50 to 55 minutes.

MAKES ONE 9-INCH CAKE.

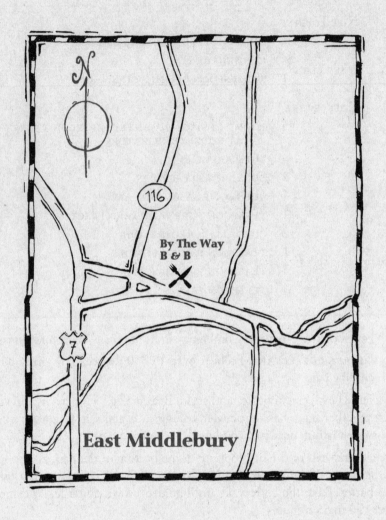

By The Way
B & B

116

7

East Middlebury

By The Way B & B

P.O. Box 264, Route 125
East Middlebury, Vermont 05740
(802) 388-6291

BY THE WAY is housed in a post-and-beam structure dating from the 1800s. The artist-owned Victorian home is filled with paintings and country antiques, and the wrap-around porch is bordered by old-fashioned flower gardens. A hearty continental breakfast is served each morning at the pine table in the dining room.

NEARBY & NOTEWORTHY: Just half a mile away, at the junction of Route 125 and Route 7, is the Middlebury Antiques Center, where a number of dealers showcase their wares.

Wild Blueberry Muffins

Maple Walnut Muffins

Wild Blueberry Muffins

1	EGG, LIGHTLY BEATEN
1	CUP MILK
2	CUPS PLUS 2 TABLESPOONS ALL-PURPOSE FLOUR
½	CUP SUGAR
3	TEASPOONS BAKING POWDER
¼	TEASPOON SALT (OPTIONAL)
1	CUP FRESH OR FROZEN WILD BLUEBERRIES
4	TABLESPOONS LIGHTLY SALTED BUTTER, MELTED

PREHEAT oven to 400 degrees F. Grease a 12-cup muffin tin.

Beat egg and milk until well combined. Sift 2 cups of the flour, sugar, baking powder and salt, if using, into a large bowl. Coat blueberries with the remaining 2 tablespoons flour. Make a well in the flour mixture. Add the egg mixture and melted butter. Stir until just combined. (The batter will be lumpy.) Gently fold in the blueberries.

Divide the batter evenly among the prepared muffin cups. Bake the muffins until golden brown and a tester comes out clean, about 20 minutes.

MAKES 12 MUFFINS.

Maple Walnut Muffins

Preparing this recipe with Grade B maple syrup gives the muffins a richer flavor.

2	CUPS ALL-PURPOSE FLOUR
1	TEASPOON BAKING POWDER
½	TEASPOON BAKING SODA
¼	TEASPOON SALT
1	CUP CHOPPED WALNUTS
2	EGGS, LIGHTLY BEATEN
½	CUP PURE MAPLE SYRUP
½	CUP MILK
4	TABLESPOONS LIGHTLY SALTED BUTTER, MELTED

PREHEAT oven to 400 degrees F. Lightly oil a 12-cup muffin tin.

Sift flour, baking powder, baking soda and salt into a large bowl. Stir in walnuts. In another bowl, beat eggs, maple syrup and milk until well combined. Make a well in the flour mixture. Add the maple syrup mixture and melted butter. Stir until just combined. (The batter will be lumpy.)

Divide the batter evenly among the prepared muffin cups. Bake the muffins until golden brown and a tester comes out clean, about 20 minutes.

MAKES 12 MUFFINS.

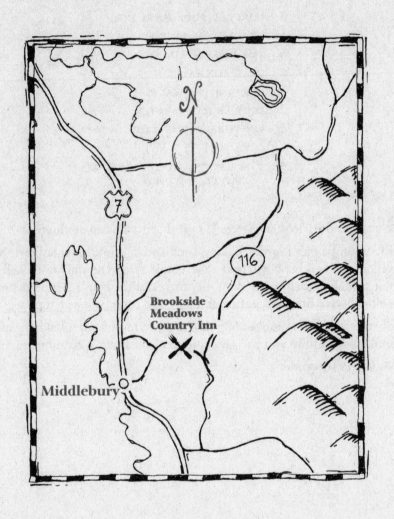

Brookside
Meadows
Country Inn

Middlebury

Brookside Meadows Country Inn

Painter Road
RD 3, Box 2460
Middlebury, Vermont 05753
(802) 388-6429/(800) 442-9887

THIS COUNTRY INN is surrounded by a 20-acre meadow bordered by a babbling brook. The view across the fields is punctuated by the ridge of the Green Mountains. The spacious lawns, perennial gardens and walking trails just outside the door truly place you in the country, yet Middlebury is just a few miles away.

NEARBY & NOTEWORTHY: If you follow scenic Happy Valley Road west and cross over Route 7, you will find yourself on Exchange Street. Otter Creek Brewing, a Vermont microbrewery, is located just off this street. Stop in for a tour of the operations and visit the retail store.

Pumpkin–Apple Streusel Muffins

Fruit & Cheese Pizza

Pumpkin–Apple Streusel Muffins

STREUSEL

4	TABLESPOONS LIGHTLY SALTED BUTTER, CUT INTO BITS
¼	CUP SUGAR
2	TABLESPOONS ALL-PURPOSE FLOUR
½	TEASPOON GROUND CINNAMON

MUFFINS

2½	CUPS ALL-PURPOSE FLOUR
2	CUPS SUGAR
1	TABLESPOON PUMPKIN PIE SPICE
1	TEASPOON BAKING SODA
½	TEASPOON SALT
2	EGGS, LIGHTLY BEATEN
1	CUP CANNED SOLID-PACK PUMPKIN
½	CUP VEGETABLE OIL
2	CUPS CHOPPED PEELED APPLES (ABOUT 3 MEDIUM)

TO PREPARE STREUSEL: Blend butter, sugar, flour and cinnamon until the mixture resembles coarse meal.

TO PREPARE MUFFINS: Preheat oven to 350 degrees F. Lightly grease 18 muffin cups in two 12-cup tins.

Combine flour, sugar, pumpkin pie spice, baking soda and salt. Beat eggs with pumpkin and oil. Add to the flour mixture and stir until just combined. Stir in apples.

Divide the batter evenly among the 18 prepared muffin cups. Fill the empty cups with water. Sprinkle the streusel over the muffins. Bake the muffins until golden brown and a tester comes out clean, 35 to 40 minutes.

MAKES 18 MUFFINS.

Fruit & Cheese Pizza

1 ROLL (20 OUNCES) SLICE-AND-BAKE
   SUGAR COOKIE DOUGH, FROZEN UNTIL FIRM

½ POUND (ONE 8-OUNCE PACKAGE) LIGHT
   CREAM CHEESE, AT ROOM TEMPERATURE

⅓ CUP SUGAR

3 TABLESPOONS BRANDY

½ TEASPOON PURE VANILLA EXTRACT

4 CUPS THINLY SLICED FRUIT (KIWIS,
   STRAWBERRIES, BANANAS)

½ CUP APRICOT PRESERVES

PREHEAT oven to 375 degrees F. Cover a 14-inch pizza pan with aluminum foil.

Cut cookie dough into ¼-inch-thick rounds and arrange in a slightly overlapping pattern on the prepared pan. Press the rounds together to seal. Bake the crust until puffed and golden brown, about 10 minutes. Let cool completely.

Combine cream cheese, sugar, 1 tablespoon of the brandy and vanilla. Spread evenly over the prepared crust. Decoratively arrange fruit slices over the cream cheese mixture.

Melt apricot preserves with the remaining 2 tablespoons brandy over low heat. Strain and brush over the fruit. Cover the pizza and chill for 1 hour before serving.

MAKES 6 SERVINGS.

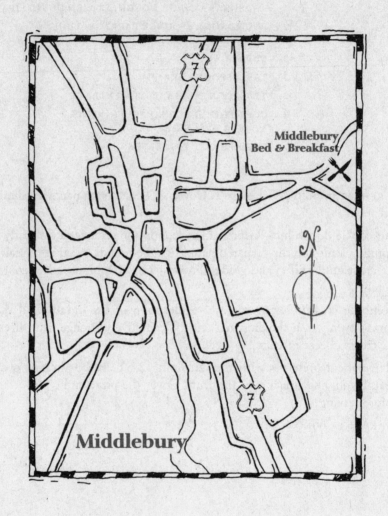

Middlebury Bed & Breakfast

7

N

7

Middlebury

Middlebury
Bed & Breakfast

Washington Street Extension
RD 1, Box 259
Middlebury, Vermont 05753
(802) 388-4851

MIDDLEBURY BED & BREAKFAST is located in a large colonial house within easy walking distance of the center of town. Despite its proximity to downtown Middlebury, it is far enough away to be quiet and peaceful. Well-behaved dogs may stay at the bed and breakfast, if they are accompanied by their owners!

NEARBY & NOTEWORTHY: The trails that wind up and down Chipman Hill (elevation 820 feet) are perfect for hikers, mountain bikers and cross-country skiers. There is an excellent view of downtown Middlebury from the bluff halfway up the hill.

Apple Bread

Lemon Poppy Seed Muffins

Zucchini–Pineapple Bread

Dog Biscuits

Apple Bread

3	EGGS, LIGHTLY BEATEN
2	CUPS SUGAR
¾	CUP VEGETABLE OIL
1	TEASPOON PURE VANILLA EXTRACT
3	CUPS ALL-PURPOSE FLOUR
1	TEASPOON BAKING POWDER
1	TEASPOON BAKING SODA
1	TEASPOON GROUND CINNAMON
1	TEASPOON GROUND NUTMEG
3	LARGE APPLES, PEELED, CORED AND CHOPPED
1	CUP ROASTED SUNFLOWER SEEDS

PREHEAT oven to 350 degrees F. Lightly oil 2 loaf pans.

Beat eggs, sugar, oil and vanilla in a large bowl. Sift together flour, baking powder, baking soda, cinnamon and nutmeg. Fold into the sugar mixture and mix until just combined. Stir in apples and sunflower seeds.

Pour the batter into the prepared loaf pans. Bake the loaves until golden brown and a tester comes out clean, about 50 minutes.

MAKES 2 LOAVES.

Lemon Poppy Seed Muffins

4	TABLESPOONS LIGHTLY SALTED BUTTER
¾	CUP SUGAR
2	EGGS
1	TEASPOON GRATED LEMON ZEST
2	CUPS ALL-PURPOSE FLOUR
2½	TEASPOONS BAKING POWDER
½	TEASPOON SALT
1	CUP MILK
3	TABLESPOONS POPPY SEEDS

PREHEAT oven to 350 degrees F. Lightly oil a 12-cup muffin tin.

In a large bowl, cream butter and sugar. Stir in eggs and lemon zest. Beat until light and fluffy. Sift together flour, baking powder and salt. Stir into the sugar mixture until just combined. Stir in milk and poppy seeds.

Divide the batter evenly among the prepared muffin cups. Bake the muffins until golden brown and a tester comes out clean, about 20 minutes.

MAKES 12 MUFFINS.

Zucchini–Pineapple Bread

2   CUPS GRATED ZUCCHINI

3   EGGS

2   CUPS SUGAR

1   CUP VEGETABLE OIL

2   TEASPOONS PURE VANILLA EXTRACT

3   CUPS ALL-PURPOSE FLOUR

2   TEASPOONS BAKING SODA

2   TEASPOONS GROUND CINNAMON

1   TEASPOON BAKING POWDER

1   TEASPOON SALT

1   TEASPOON GROUND NUTMEG

1   CAN (20 OUNCES) CRUSHED PINEAPPLE, PACKED IN JUICE, DRAINED

1   CUP ROASTED SUNFLOWER SEEDS

PREHEAT oven to 350 degrees F. Lightly oil 2 loaf pans.

Place zucchini in a colander. Let stand for a few minutes and press with a small plate to remove moisture.

Beat eggs, sugar, oil and vanilla in a large bowl until well combined. Sift together flour, baking soda, cinnamon, baking powder, salt and nutmeg. Fold into the egg mixture and stir until just combined. Stir in the zucchini, pineapple and sunflower seeds.

Pour the batter into the prepared loaf pans. Bake the loaves until golden brown and a tester comes out clean, about 1 hour.

MAKES 2 LOAVES.

Dog Biscuits

1½	CUPS ALL-PURPOSE FLOUR
1½	CUPS WHOLE WHEAT FLOUR
1	CUP RYE FLOUR
1	CUP CORNMEAL
¼	CUP LIVER POWDER (AVAILABLE AT HEALTH-FOOD STORES)
¼	CUP BONE MEAL (AVAILABLE AT HEALTH-FOOD STORES)
1	TEASPOON SALT
1	TEASPOON GARLIC POWDER
1	CAN (10.5 OUNCES) BEEF BROTH
½	CUP VEGETABLE OIL
1	EGG

PREHEAT oven to 200 degrees F. Lightly oil baking sheets.

Mix together flours, cornmeal, liver powder, bone meal, salt and garlic powder. Stir in beef broth, oil and egg. Mix well.

Roll out the dough to a thickness of ¼ inch on a lightly floured surface. Cut out shapes with 4-inch cookie cutters and set on the prepared baking sheets. Bake the biscuits until hard, about 2 hours.

MAKES ABOUT 50 BISCUITS.

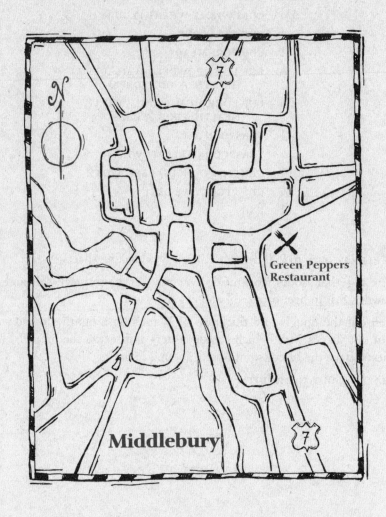

Green Peppers
Restaurant

Middlebury

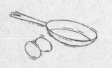

Green Peppers Restaurant

Washington Street
Middlebury, Vermont 05753
(802) 388-3164

GREEN PEPPERS RESTAURANT is an informal eatery well known for its pizzas, salads and grinders. Doughs are prepared daily from scratch as are many of the soups, dressings and sauces. Vermont Cheddar, Vermont mozzarella and other Vermont products are used whenever possible. Eat in or grab something to take out and walk to the Green for a picnic.

NEARBY & NOTEWORTHY: You can even factor in a history lesson on your visit—the 1810 Middlebury jail is located just opposite the restaurant, though it is now disguised as a private home with commercial space. The stone jail was built to replace the original jail, just several doors to its west, when the number of prisoners exceeded the prison's capacity. Ironically, the original jail is now occupied by a law firm.

Green Salad with Italian Dressing

Pasta with Tomato Sauce

Green Salad with Italian Dressing

¾   CUP OLIVE OIL

¼   CUP RED WINE VINEGAR

      JUICE OF 1 LEMON

1   TEASPOON DRIED OREGANO

1   TEASPOON SUGAR

      SALT & GROUND BLACK PEPPER

12   CUPS WASHED, DRIED AND TORN ROMAINE LETTUCE

IN A LARGE salad bowl, whisk together oil, vinegar, lemon juice, oregano and sugar. Season with salt and pepper to taste. Add romaine and toss well.

MAKES 6 SERVINGS.

Pasta with Tomato Sauce

3	CLOVES GARLIC, FINELY CHOPPED
2	TABLESPOONS OLIVE OIL
2	LARGE SPANISH ONIONS, CHOPPED
1	MEDIUM GREEN BELL PEPPER, CHOPPED
2	CANS (28 OUNCES EACH) CRUSHED TOMATOES
2	TEASPOONS GROUND BLACK PEPPER
2	TEASPOONS DRIED THYME LEAVES
2	TEASPOONS DRIED OREGANO
1	TEASPOON SALT
1	BAY LEAF
1½	POUNDS LINGUINE OR FETTUCCINE

IN A LARGE heavy saucepan, sauté garlic in oil until fragrant but not browned. Add onions and bell peppers and sauté until very soft, about 30 minutes. Add tomatoes, pepper, thyme, oregano, salt and bay leaf. Simmer for 1 hour. Discard the bay leaf.

Boil linguine or fettuccine in salted water until al dente, 8 to 10 minutes. Drain. Spoon the sauce over the linguine.

MAKES 6 SERVINGS.

Recipe Index

S

SALAD(s)
Baby Field Greens with Olive
Paste Crostini, 94
Black Bean & Rice, with
Grilled Shrimp, 32
Chicken, Smoked, with Walnut
Dressing, 125
Goat Cheese, Cornmeal-
Crusted, 130
Gracianne, 83
Green Bean, with Tuna
Sauce, 139
Green, with Dried Fruits &
Maple Vinaigrette, 154
Green, with Italian
Dressing, 180
Lettuce & Red Cabbage, 119
Shrimp Caesar, Warm, with
Three Relishes, 55-56
Stellar, 36-37
Village Greens, 17

SALAD DRESSING(s). See also
Vinaigrette(s)
Italian, with Green Salad, 180
Walnut, with Smoked Chicken
Salad, 125

SALMON
Dip, Sour Cream, 116
Spread, 137
with Strawberry & Black
Peppercorn Vinaigrette, 72

SALSA, Mango, with Grilled
Swordfish, 155

SAUCE(s)
Chocolate, with Peanut Pie,
Frozen, 51
Corn & Sweet Pepper, with

New England Crab Cakes, 70
Herbal Cream, with Lamb
Chops, 126
Horseradish, Sweet, with Dirty
Steak, 38
Raspberry, with Chocolate
Pizza Cookie, 127
Red Wine & Gorgonzola, with
Grilled Venison, 71
Tomato, with Pasta, 181
Tuna, with Green Bean
Salad, 139

SAUSAGE
Frittata, California, 102

SCALLOPS
Seafood Bisque, 124
Seafood Gratinée, 18

SCONES
Walnut Chocolate Chip, 45
Walnut & Currant, 88

SEAFOOD. See also Crab(meat);
Fish; Lobster; Salmon;
Shrimp; Swordfish
Bisque, 124
Brunch Bake, 162
Gratinée, 18

SESAME SEED
Bread, 120
Bread, Honey Oatmeal, 131

SHAKE, Fruit, 160

SHELLFISH. See Crab(meat);
Lobster; Seafood; Shrimp

SHERBET, Brandied, 121

SHRIMP
Caesar Salad, Warm, with
Three Relishes, 55-56